THE CLANDESTINE MARRIAGE

THE CLANDESTINE MARRIAGE

By David Garrick & George Coleman the elder

Together with two short plays

THE CUNNING MAN
by Charles Burney after Jean Jacques Rousseau

&

THE REHEARSAL OR,
BAYES IN PETTYCOATS
by Catherine Clive

edited by Noel Chevalier

broadview literary texts

Canadian Cataloguing in Publication Data
Main entry under title:
The clandestine marriage and other plays
(Broadview literary texts).
ISBN 1-55111-027-X
Contents: The clandestine marriage / David Garrick,
George Colman the Elder — The cunning-man /
Charles Burney after Jean-Jacques Rousseau — The
rehearsal, or Bayes in petticoats / Catherine Clive

1. English Drama — 18th Century.   I.   Chevalier, Noel, 1963–
II.   Colman, George, 1732–1794.
The clandestine marriage.   III.   Burney, Charles,
1726–1814. The cunning-man.   IV.   Clive, Catherine
Raftor, 1711–1785. The rehearsal, or Bayes in
petticoats.   V.   Series.

PR1269.C53   1995   822'.608   C95-930751-6

Broadview Press
P.O. Box 1243, Peterborough, Ontario, Canada, K9J 7H5

in the United States of America
3576 California Road, Orchard Park, NY 14127

in the United Kingdom:
B.R.A.D. Book Representation & Distribution Ltd., 244A, London Road,
Hadleigh, Essex SS7 2DE

Broadview Press gratefully acknowledges the support of the Canada Council, the Ontario Arts Council, the Ontario Publishing Centre, and the Ministry of Canadian Heritage.

PRINTED IN CANADA

10 9 8 7 6 5 4 3 2 1   95 96 97 98

Contents

Preface

This new edition of three eighteenth-century comedies began while I was researching material for my doctoral thesis on Christopher Smart. When Smart was confined in a private asylum, Garrick staged a revival of Aaron Hill's blank-verse tragedy *Merope*, and added as an afterpiece an original farce, *The Guardian*. I read both these plays, hoping to find some significance in Garrick's choice, but none was immediately apparent. Nonetheless, I was intrigued by the idea that eighteenth-century audiences were quite prepared to see a stiff, classical tragedy and a light, modern farce in the same evening. I began to read more afterpieces, particularly those by Smart's friend, Arthur Murphy, and I was struck by how funny and accessible these plays are. Although they lack the sophisticated wit and intricate plotting of the best Restoration plays, they avoid the unbearable sentimentality of some eighteenth-century comedy and of nineteenth-century melodrama. And while there are many anthologies of eighteenth-century mainpieces, and a few anthologies of afterpieces, there is no anthology I know of that tries to combine the two in one volume. This combination shows the reader something of what a typical eighteenth-century theatre evening was like.

Two of the plays in this volume – *The Clandestine Marriage* and *The Cunning-Man* – were actually presented together on a number of nights during the 1766-67 season. The third play, Catherine Clive's *Bayes in Petticoats*, was written earlier, and so technically falls outside my original idea of the volume as one unit that corresponds to an actual eighteenth-century theatre evening. I decided to include Clive's play for a number of reasons: first, because the contributions of eighteenth-century women playwrights is still woefully under-represented in modern editions; second, because Clive herself was a prominent member of the Drury Lane company, and created one of the main roles in *The Clandestine Marriage*, Mrs. Heidelberg; and finally, because the farce develops a critical perspective on pastoral that links it to both *The Clandestine Marriage* and *The Cunning-Man*. I explain my understanding of the pastoral motif in all three plays in the Introduction.

This edition will, I hope, stimulate further interest in eighteenth-century stage practices: ideally, I would hope that a theatre company would present an eighteenth-century "double feature," even if only to revive some very good comic writing. Unfortunately, the limitations of this project could not allow me to include the music, or suggest the staging of the plays, but developments in multimedia technology might make electronic editions easily available in the not-too-distant future.

I would like to extend my thanks to Don LePan, president of Broadview Press, for listening to my idea and giving me the opportunity to bring this edition to light. Thanks also to Linda Steele, to George Kirkpatrick and to Fred Graver for their invaluable assistance.

Thanks are also due to the helpful and friendly staff at numerous libraries: the Main Library, Special Collections Division, Music Library, Sedgwick Library, and Wilson Recording Collection at the University of British Columbia; the Main Library, Special Collections room, and Fine Arts Library at the University of Regina; Luther College Library; the British Library; and the libraries at Queen's University, University of Alberta, University of Calgary, and Yale University.

Many others helped with this project, even if only to hear my ideas and to offer encouragement: Richard Bevis, Tom Blom, Alan Brody, Judy Dorn, Robert Eggleston, James Nielson, Craig Poile, Peter Sabor, Libby Smigel, and Christopher Smith. To them I extend my sincere thanks.

Finally, I would also like to express my gratitude to my wife and colleague, Dorothy Lane, whose hard work, dedication to perfection, and impeccable scholarship are always an inspiration. Without her support during a tough year, this edition would never have been completed.

Introduction

An Evening's Entertainment

The three plays in this volume were all written for and performed at Drury Lane Theatre under the direction of David Garrick between 1750 and 1766. *The Clandestine Marriage* and *The Cunning-Man* appeared on the same bill during the 1766-67 season, and form one of the combinations of mainpiece and afterpiece that were standard stage practice throughout the eighteenth century. The texts display a wide range of influences, and reveal something of the variety of entertainment available at Drury Lane. *The Clandestine Marriage* has its roots in satirical comedy and in the pastoral tradition; *The Cunning-Man* is Charles Burney's translation and adaptation of *Le Devin du village* (1752), a pastoral musical interlude by Jean-Jacques Rousseau. The final play, *The Rehearsal* – or *Bayes in Petticoats*, as it is more commonly known to distinguish it from George Villiars, Duke of Buckingham's original *Rehearsal* (1671) – was written by the most versatile and celebrated actress in Garrick's company, Catherine Clive. She also created the role of Mrs. Heidelberg in *The Clandestine Marriage*. Its inclusion in this volume calls attention to the contributions of female playwrights during this period, since a significant number of women wrote both mainpieces and afterpieces that were performed at Drury Lane. Clive's play, in fact, highlights the difficulty many of these women had in being taken seriously as writers.

This collection of eighteenth-century plays is the first to consider the relationship between mainpiece and afterpieces by different playwrights in the same volume. The aim of the collection is not simply to reprint a representative anthology of plays, but to imitate "an evening's entertainment" as audiences in Garrick's time might have experienced it. The reader will have a better understanding of the context in which eighteenth-century plays were performed. Naturally, a printed text cannot reproduce the experience of the theatre: much of the improvised stage-business that often ensures a play's success is missing, and the sounds and appearance of the theatre must be left to the reader's own imagination. Moreover, eighteenth-century plays were often revised – sometimes quite heavily – before they were printed. But even the printed versions of these plays allow both students of theatre and general readers alike to gain a sound understanding of the contexts of Georgian stage comedy.

To understand the context of the plays, one must begin with Garrick himself. The extent of Garrick's influence on the character of the eighteenth-century stage cannot be underestimated. Much of what theatregoers experienced at Drury Lane from 1747 to well into the nineteenth century can be attributed to Garrick's strong personal vision of the theatre. To a certain extent, Garrick was controlled by the demands of tradition, but his real genius lay in his ability to respond to public taste and to calculate public readiness for innovation. When he was successful, he transformed stage practice and stage traditions and made Drury Lane the most important theatre of his day; when he was unsuccessful, the results were disastrous.[1]

Garrick had not been born into an acting family; his father was an officer in James Tyrrel's Regiment of Dragoons. When Garrick moved to London, he initially began law studies at Lincoln's Inn; later, he set up a wine business with his brother Peter. Untrained as an actor, his acting style did not conform to the complex conventions that governed the representation of character on the stage. According to seventeenth-century theorists, acting consisted of encoding the psychological interactions between individuals within a set of stylized gestures and facial expressions. The actor's interpretation of a role depended largely on his or her reading of what conventions were required by the text: love, fear, rage, delight, and so on. Garrick, following a style pioneered by Covent Garden actor Charles Macklin, adopted a more naturalistic approach to acting, combining conventional gestures and expressions with those that seemed more to represent the reactions of a particular individual psyche. He also practiced modulations in his delivery that approached natural speech. Thus, each character appeared more individuated, more like a real, knowable human being.

Garrick's acting style was immediately popular with audiences, although Colley Cibber's more traditional style at Covent Garden was no less popular: audiences accommodated themselves to a number of different styles. Within seven years of his first stage appearance he had taken over management of Drury Lane, a position he continued to hold until 1776. During his tenure as manager he renovated the theatre no fewer than nine times. He expanded the seating capacity and experimented with lighting so as to allow the audience the maximum opportunity to observe the subtleties of his facial expressions. In twenty-nine years he made Drury Lane into the most important playhouse in England.

The repertory at both patent houses remained competitive during Garrick's tenure as manager. Both houses offered a balanced mixture of tragedy, comedy and farce. Garrick, however, provided more new plays each season than Covent Garden, according to the records of *The London Stage*, and was more willing to risk experimental afterpieces. Perhaps the most significant achievements of the Drury Lane repertory under Garrick were his revisions of the standard performing texts of Elizabethan and Jacobean plays, particularly Shakespeare's. Garrick restored much to the original texts that had been obliterated from Restoration versions. The most important of his adaptations were *King Lear* (1756), which began to wean audiences away from the more familiar version by Nahum Tate, and *The Tempest* (1773), which for years had been performed as an opera with a libretto by William Davenant and John Dryden. At the same time, he carefully edited plays such as *Richard III* and *Hamlet* – plays that had become popular largely because of his interpretations of the title roles – to quicken the action, and to increase their accessibility to an audience seeking delight rather than instruction.

Garrick approached his texts as an entertainer and theatre manager, not as a literary scholar. His audience expected literate, witty scripts that could serve as useful vehicles for the talents of the resident acting company. Harry William Pedicord and Frederick L. Bergmann, editors of the standard edition of Garrick's plays, note that *The Clandestine Marriage* was "conceived...in terms of actual stage personalities than in terms of stock characters of literary tradition" (419). While this assertion is not entirely accurate – most of the characters in the play have precedents in traditional stage comedy – it is clear from the manuscript drafts that Garrick and Colman constructed the comedy to show the best talents of the cast.

The talents of Drury Lane also excelled in presenting afterpieces. This was no small achievement: no study of theatre of the period can ignore the importance of afterpieces, especially considering the proportion of afterpieces to mainpieces composed during the period. Richard Bevis calculates that "of the plays received by the Licencer between 1737 and 1777 nearly 80 per cent were afterpieces of one type or another" (*Afterpieces* xiv). Clearly, to look only to the full-length plays produced during this period is to miss out on some of the most interesting and important works produced during the century. Some of the best comic writing of the period can be found in these afterpieces. Playwrights evidently felt more comfortable with the tighter structure and smaller scope that the afterpiece demanded. Actors, on the other hand, were given more range for improvisation in afterpieces, and did not have to subsume their comic talents to the demands of a fully-plotted five-act piece. Although the tone of these plays is invariably light, the best afterpieces are commentaries on manners.

The practice of offering double bills in English theatre dates back to the Restoration stage, although the afterpiece had been a staple of the French stage since about 1650. Pedicord has suggested (*Theatrical Public* 36-39) that a second feature was necessary, given that a significant share of the audience was unavailable to spend a full evening at the theatre. For the leisured classes, an evening's entertainment could begin in the afternoon: the house would open as early as three o'clock – the beginning of the dinner hour – and performances began at five o'clock (in Garrick's time, the first curtain would go up at six o'clock). Those who wished to linger over dinner would send servants to purchase tickets and occupy choice seats until they arrived.

These distinguished theatre patrons constituted only about three per cent of the population of London. The vast majority of the population – journeyman labourers, farmers, paupers, and vagrants – had neither the time nor the money to spend watching plays. However, about 12 per cent of London inhabitants did have the money, but were unable to quit work as early as five o'clock to secure themselves seats at the theatre. M. Dorothy George, in *London Life in the Eighteenth Century*, calculates that most tradespeople did not finish work until as late as nine, by which time the mainpiece and interlude music would be well over. In order to capture a market that had enough disposable income to spend on theatrical entertainment, theatre managers allowed latecomers half-price admission provided they came at the end of the third act of the mainpiece. Thus for half the regular admission price a theatregoer could enjoy part of the mainpiece, a musical interlude that featured singers, dancers, or new concert pieces, and a short farce. Performances generally concluded by 10 p.m.

Those who attended afterpieces witnessed most of the new dramatic energies of the period. A study of the records of *The London Stage* reveals that by far most of the mainpieces produced during a season were revivals of older plays. As the century wore on, managers were increasingly reluctant to stage new full-length plays since the costs of mounting them required only hits from playwrights.[2] Although Garrick insisted that financial expediency was never a consideration in his decision to stage new works – any play worth producing was worth spending money to produce – he nevertheless had to be careful about what he deemed worth spending money on. If a new mainpiece were "damned" by the audience, the theatre had to be prepared to play whatever the audience called for as an alternative. Eighteenth-century audiences were extremely volatile, and sometimes started riots if they felt the management was not catering to their demands. Audience expectation, combined with the time and expense involved in mounting new five-act pieces, meant that both patent houses relied heavily on their large repertory to keep themselves financially solvent, and reserved innovation for smaller, less ambitious productions.[3]

Most of Garrick's own dramatic writing consisted of afterpieces. While Garrick's plays were not as highly polished as those of Arthur Murphy, Samuel Foote, or even his own collaborator, George Colman, Garrick nevertheless knew how to write popular pieces that succeeded more on the stage than the page. For example, he revised his most successful farce, *Lethe*, six times between 1740 and 1772, to add and delete characters, and to keep its humour contemporary.

Finally, as *The Cunning-Man*, the burletta in *Bayes in Petticoats* and even the Epilogue to *The Clandestine Marriage* prove, one cannot ignore the importance of music on the eighteenth-century stage: more than half of all afterpieces employ some form of music or dancing. As an alternative to full-scale opera – generally performed exclusively at the Royal opera house, Haymarket – Drury Lane and Covent Garden offered genres such as the burletta, ballad opera, musical farce, revue, and even burlesque. At other theatres, various musical burlesque shows dominated the stage. For example, Christopher Smart's *Old Woman's Oratory* (1750-c.1763) parodied the declamatory style of dissenting preacher John "Orator" Henley, and featured novelty acts such as performing animals, one-legged dancers, and take-offs of Italian opera singers.

Seen in this context, the afterpiece significantly expands the variety of entertainment featured on the London stage. Bevis has argued that the preponderance of "sentimental" comedy in eighteenth-century drama is balanced by the vast numbers of "laughing" afterpieces. The importance of both traditions is apparent when seen in context: audiences did not necessarily choose between "laughing" and "sentimental" comedies, since often both were featured on the same evening. Such a strict division between genres is largely a critical construct: the evidence of the plays themselves and the context of their performance show that audiences preferred the generic miscellany to an evening composed of only one form of entertainment.

To read the plays within their original context is to share in the interplay of meaning derived from the juxtaposition of texts. Recontextualization allows important hermeneutic opportunities that would not be otherwise available, not only at the broader level of cultural studies, but at the level of close textual reading as well. There is no evidence that mainpieces were linked with afterpieces according to any strict plan. Yet context affects audience reception, and this fact Garrick knew as well as any theatre manager. One way of reading a play may be suggested by the play with which it is performed; some mainpieces and afterpieces play better together than others. The reading of the three plays that I offer here derives in part from my reading of them as a single volume: I have looked for a common thematic thread that runs through all three plays.

The Clandestine Marriage and *The Cunning-Man* both explore ideas commonly found in pastoral writing; *The Cunning-Man* itself is a pastoral interlude. Both plays explore the tension between city and country life, and both assert the superiority of the latter. *Bayes in Petticoats* is less overtly an example of pastoral *per se*, but Mrs. Hazard's choice of a pastoral burletta as her new play, and that play's disdainful reception by the town wits, clearly seems to be another version of the same theme. I explore the pastoral tradition and the place of these three plays more fully later. My choice of these two afterpieces to accompany *The Clandestine Marriage* has directed one particular reading of the play: other combinations are certainly possible, and the complex relationship between mainpieces and afterpieces in eighteenth-century theatre is an area that would well repay further study.

Stage Tradition and the Pastoral

The traditions of pastoral on the stage date back to Elizabethan comedy, with Shakespeare's *As You Like It* perhaps the best-known example. Pastoral was an important genre in Elizabethan literature, but by the eighteenth century its conventions seemed stale. John Gay saw pastoral conventions as a fair target for satire, and parodied them in his poem-cycle *The Shepherd's Week* (1713) and in *The Beggar's Opera* (1728).[4]

Pastoral is the genre of pleasure. Elizabethan pastoral celebrates a life of retirement from political intrigue, from the dangers and temptations of court life. Its central character is the rustic – the shepherd and shepherdess – who is able to speak eloquently about simple pleasures. In the conventions of the genre, the rough primitivism of pastoral life is seen as a harmonic co-existence with Nature, and the rustic is presented as better off than the courtier, simply because rustic life is uncomplicated and uncorrupted by the world.

The pastoral ideal fascinated writers of the century. Gay attacked not so much the ideal itself as the conventions that expressed it. Much satirical writing of the period censured the vanity and greed of city life, as represented either by the "Titles" – the nobility, who generally inhabited London's West End – or the "Cits" – the mercantile class, who generally lived within the limits of the City proper.

By the eighteenth century, therefore, the term "pastoral" had gained respectability not so much as a literary genre but as a perspective on Augustan class structure: a discourse that permits social commentary.[5] Paul Alpers, in exploring what he calls "the anecdote" of pastoral, asserts that pastoral is not a landscape or a set of conventional characters (i.e. shepherds), but rather "an interpretation or development or use of the representative anecdote of shepherds' lives" (457). According to Alpers, shepherds themselves are representative of human experience, and therefore

the dramatis personae of pastoral can be extended to include other rustics or socially inferior persons on the grounds that

they are the equivalent, in a given society or world, of shepherds, or that they more truly have the representative status
that traditional pastoral ascribes to its herdsmen. (456)

Andrew V. Ettin argues that pastoral motifs extend outside of traditional pastoral literature. He cites Schiller's *Kaballe und Liebe* (1782)
as an example of "a bourgeois tragedy" that underlines the same basic premise and shows the same basic values as traditional pastoral.
Pastoral stands for a way of life that rejects the values of the upper
classes, and asserts the simple, homespun rustic values: "For the
writer who respects pastoral values," Ettin argues, "the things of the
country might not be good enough to win the respect of refined
urbanites, but they are too precious to be squandered on those who
cannot or will not appreciate their special qualities" (*Literature and
the Pastoral* 64). In this way, *The Clandestine Marriage* can be considered a "bourgeois pastoral," because the representatives of the pastoral ideal, Lovewell and Fanny, are both members of the middle
class, yet reject both the "City," mercantile values of Sterling and
the aristocratic values of Lord Ogleby and Sir John.

Whereas Gay had satirized pastoral convention, and attempted
to show in characters with names such as "Grubbinol" and "Blow-
zelinda" the essential coarseness of country life, the three plays in
this volume all use the pastoral ideal as a confirmation of moral – if
not physical or social – superiority of the rustic world. The prob-
lem at the outset of both *The Cunning-Man* and the burletta in
Bayes in Petticoats is the same: a young "swain," (Colin, Corydon)
has rejected his lover (Phœbe, Miranda) for a wealthier – and hence
more attractive – rival. The issue for both women is how to persuade the swain to reaffirm the pastoral ideal by recognising the
true value of his rustic lover.

As a pastoral, *The Cunning-Man* follows *The Clandestine Marriage*
quite easily. Burney's interlude underlines the ideal represented by
Lovewell and Fanny in the mainpiece. The play opens with Phœbe
(Colette in Rousseau's original), who is lamenting that her beloved
Colin has left her for a more fashionable woman. She decides to
visit the village wise-man (the *devin*, or soothsayer, of the title),
who instructs her to act indifferent in order to win Colin again.
The cunning-man's "magic" derives more from his understanding
of human nature than from any magic, and the play includes a

mock conjuring-trick that gently satirises the rustic's belief in magic.

Like most pastorals, *The Cunning-Man* asserts the superiority of the retired, country life over the fashionable world. Colin is presented as a mere dupe of a fashionable nymph, and the play ends with an extended country dance that affirms Colin and Phœbe's place within the rustic setting. The resolution of the play is possible in part because the rusticity of both setting and characters is strongly evoked. For the cunning-man to effect his reunion of Colin and Phœbe, he must rely in part on the natural setting. Both Rousseau and Burney are well aware of the tradition that underlines the setting of the play: Sidney's *Arcadia* (1593) provides the archetype of the pastoral setting as a space where the moral failings of the more sophisticated world can be corrected.

The Clandestine Marriage provides a bourgeois version of the same archetype in the form of Sterling's landscape garden. The eighteenth-century landscape garden was the gentrified version of Arcadia. By mid-century the trend in landscaping had moved away from the formal, neo-classical garden to the artificial wildernesses designed by Lancelot "Capability" Brown (1715–83). Brown's genius lay in his ability to transform vast tracts of private parkland into an organically unified landscape, a prospect whose best views could be seen from the main house. Sterling's garden in *The Clandestine Marriage* is a satirical version of such a garden, since Sterling has neither the land nor the taste to match the gardens of larger estates.

Garrick and Colman use the setting of the play to extend the satire on the mercantile mind. Within Sterling's landscape-garden the authors satirise contemporary taste and manner, since Sterling's pride in his garden is considerably greater than his guests' admiration of it. But the satire on fashions in gardening is less significant than the signifying power of the garden itself. The garden is a politically important space, since it is Sterling's petty-bourgeois version of the great landed estates he wants to emulate. Garrick and Colman draw a direct connection between landscape as conceived by both the landed gentry (Lord Ogleby) and those aspiring to gentrification (Sterling, Mrs. Heidelberg and Betsey Sterling) and, by implication, moral deficiency. By the same token, the two lovers, Fanny and Lovewell, must transcend Sterling's garden, both literally and metaphorically, if their alternative to Sterling's bourgeois ideal is to be made real.

The scenes in which Sir John declares his love for Fanny to Lovewell, and in which Lord Ogleby becomes convinced of Fanny's love for him both take place in Sterling's garden. The garden is therefore the centrepiece of Sterling's country house, and the central focus of the play. It is conceived on a grand scale, but in bad taste – the epitome of bourgeois attempts at grandeur. Sterling has planned his garden as a deliberate pastiche of what he understands to be the pastoral ideal. As he boasts to Lord Ogleby, he has transformed "wild" nature into an artificial conception of "the country":

> This is quite another-guess sort of place than it was when I first took it, my Lord. We were surrounded with trees. I cut down above fifty to make the lawn before the house and let in the wind and the sun – smack-smooth – as you see. – Then I made a greenhouse out of the old laundry, and turned the brew-house into a pinery. – The high octagon summer-house, you see yonder, is raised on the mast of a ship, given me by an East India captain who has turned many a thousand of my money. It commands the whole road. (II.ii. 44-53)

Even Sterling's sister, herself a great pretender to gentility but usually contemptuous of her brother's lack of fashion, has also joined the scheme: her contribution has been to renovate "a little gothick dairy." Flirting with Lord Ogleby, she invites him to this dairy to join her in a suitably rustic "sullabub warm from the cow." Finally, Lord Ogleby notices a steeple, which he takes to be the parish church. Sterling, however, is proud to correct him:

> It is no church at all, my Lord! It is a spire that I have built against a tree, a field or two off, to terminate the prospect. One must always have a church, or an obelisk, or a some-thing, to terminate the prospect, you know. That's a rule in taste, my Lord. (II.ii. 117-21)

Sterling's country estate, therefore, is a faux-pastoral, since it conforms more to arbitrary rules of taste than to any real country landscape.

Sterling's obsession with landscaping and his obvious bad taste are echoes of Alexander Pope's dictates on taste in his "Epistle to Burlington." Pope notes that, amid the excesses of Timon's villa, Timon himself, the possessor of the garden, seems to disappear. For all its grandeur, the garden has a diminishing quality about it, quite opposite to the effect intended by its owner:

Who but must laugh, the Master when he sees,
A puny insect, shiv'ring at a breeze!
Lo, what huge heaps of littleness around!
The whole, a labour'd Quarry above ground.
...
My Lord advances with majestic mien,
Smit with the mighty pleasure to be seen.
(ll. 107-10; 127-28)

Pope's comments here serve as a fitting epigram to Sterling's taste.

Yet Sterling's ideas, ridiculous though they seem here, are underwritten by the mercantile culture within which he moves. Although he wants to demonstrate his familiarity with modish landscaping, he is mainly motivated by an ethic of conspicuous consumption that ironically reinforces the notion of bourgeois pastoral as antithetical to nature. The church-spire is a marker of the extent of Sterling's lands; it "terminates the prospect," but it also shows to Sterling's distinguished guests just how much land is his to control. The central meaning of Sterling's garden is not nature, but property, or nature commodified. In this highly significant space Sterling's daughter, Fanny, is also seen as a property or commodity. Moreover, the extent to which Sterling will be able to commodify her successfully will threaten what has already been established as a "natural" union, the marriage between Lovewell and Fanny that has resulted from love, not economics.

Sterling's garden also represents another aspect of bourgeois life that clearly sets it apart from the landed gentry. Sterling, as a man of business, wants to make his garden busy. The land itself functions as a sign of conspicuous consumption. Some aspects of the garden, such as the fish in the pond, are meant to be literally consumed. At the same time, the garden violates one principle of true pastoral, which is the impression of spaciousness, of limitless land and vast prospect. Sterling is obviously proud of his "close walks," and remarks to Lord Ogleby that, in conformity with modish taste, "here's none of your strait lines here, but all taste – zig-zag – crinkum-crankum – in and out – right and left – to and again – twisting and turning like a worm" (II.ii. 76-78). Lord Ogleby answers that Sterling is "a most excellent economist of [his] land," and notes that the whole garden "lies together in as small parcels as if it was placed in pots out at your window in Gracechurch-Street" (II.ii. 82-84). Sterling, therefore, has simply carried his city conception of landscape into the country, and has substituted bourgeois space-saving for aristocratic spaciousness.

Sterling's winding walks and his narrow conception of landscape are bourgeois reductions of the kind of vast estate conceived by the landed gentry. In large estates the winding walks force the viewer's perspective, and act as frames for the most breathtaking prospects. The ideals that Sterling misses do exist in a garden such as Pemberley in *Pride and Prejudice*. Jane Austen's description of Pemberley reveals the vastness of Darcy's estate; the amount of land Darcy possesses is one factor in Elizabeth Bennett's reassessment of him. Pemberley, too, has winding walks, but the twists and turns are not there simply to conform to modish taste; they are carefully planned to reveal the extent of Darcy's land-holdings:

> ˙ They entered the woods, and bidding adieu to the river for a while, ascended some of the higher grounds; whence, in spots where the opening of the trees gave the eye power to wander, were many charming views of the valley, the opposite hills, with the long range of woods overspreading many, and occasionally part of the stream. Mr. Gardiner expressed a wish of going round the whole Park, but feared it might be beyond a walk. With a triumphant smile, they were told, that it was ten miles round. (223)

Pemberley, as landscape, is a sign of its owner's wealth; but its carefully constructed wildness reveals its owner's taste, since the prospects possess an aesthetic dimension that transcends Sterling's tacky pastiche.

If Sterling's garden is faux-pastoral, then the ideals that the garden represents are false as well. In Sterling's view, the landscape garden is a sign of its owner's taste and financial success: so, too, are the marriages he contracts. Sterling clearly regards himself as superior to the landed gentry, since many who have "birth and education" are also in need of money – as we learn is true of Sir John Melvil and Lord Ogleby. Sterling's delight in his entertaining these two is his ability to show off his wealth, and he crows the he will "shew your fellows at the other end of the town how we live in the city. They shall eat gold – and drink gold – and lie in gold" (I.i. 257-59).

Sterling's gross mishandling of his landscape garden shows a fundamental flaw in his understanding of the pastoral idiom. Like many, he believes pastoral to be synonymous with landscape; that is, he believes that he can impose a picture of an Arcadian, idyllic world into an essentially bourgeois setting simply by redefining the land. Sterling's bourgeois values tell him that money can let him have things both ways: he can have both instant gentility, by marrying his daughters off to impoverished nobles, and instant rusticity, by paying out lavish sums for his fake spires and "improved" ruins.

Garrick and Colman do more here than poke fun at fashionable taste in landscape. The garden-setting of the play suggests a space where the pastoral ideal cannot be achieved, and indeed, can even be threatened: both Lovewell's and Lord Ogleby's attempted seductions of Fanny take place in the garden. Lovewell and Fanny's hidden marriage – what Betsey contemptuously dismisses as "love and a cottage" – is actually the real counterpart of the ideals suggested by Sterling's garden. The marriage is marked by its lack of attachment to any real estate. It is technically illegal; therefore, neither Lovewell nor Fanny can lay claim to any inheritance or even dower gift from any member of Sterling's house. When we consider that Sir John is willing to offer even the reduced rate of £50,000 instead of £80,000, for Fanny, Fanny's decision to marry the impoverished Lovewell is a decision to throw away a fortune.

At the same time, any dwelling place is necessarily a hindrance to the couple, since legally Fanny is obliged to live under her father's roof and not to seek one with Lovewell. This hindrance is all the more grave since Fanny is pregnant and she cannot hide her condition much longer. Family, property, and title are all bars to Lovewell and Fanny; they have consciously chosen to reject these, but Garrick and Colman ask us to accept their choice as more desirable than Betsey's choice to marry Sir John Melvil. One of the dictates of sentimental comedy asserts that marriage for love is always to be preferred to marriage for title or property.

Lovewell and Fanny attempt to live in a world of their own making, a world that aspires to the pastoral ideals of retirement and freedom from material wealth. *The Clandestine Marriage* is a bourgeois reworking of the pastoral idiom, with an impoverished clerk and a beautiful younger daughter acting as the replacements for the swain and shepherdess of traditional pastoral. Moreover, Garrick and Colman suggest that the pastiche of pastoral stereotypes in Sterling's garden has nothing whatever to do with pastoral as newly-defined by Lovewell and Fanny. Sterling's landscape garden is a fake archaism, a mercantile version of a Golden World that pays too much attention to the Gold.

Garrick and Colman avoid taking the political implications of the play too far, partly because to do so would be to spoil the comedy, and partly because the radical political version of pastoral explored by Blake in *Songs of Innocence* and *The Book of Thel*, Wordsworth in *Lyrical Ballads*, and Goethe in his early lyrics is of no concern to the playwrights. Garrick was particularly sensitive to the demands of his audience; moreover, the Licensing Act had expressly forbidden political theatre. Political satire is not Garrick's (or Colman's) idiom: he is careful to resolve the illegitimacy of Fanny's and Lovewell's marriage through the sanction of Lord Ogleby. That sanction reasserts the power of the aristocracy, and exonerates the playwrights from any politically subversive motives.

Consequently, *The Clandestine Marriage* is most often played as a comedy that showcases the talents of character-actors. It is, however, more than that: if we laugh at Sterling's ostentatiousness and his obsession with money or Mrs. Heidelberg's ruthless social climbing, and if we applaud Fanny's and Lovewell's efforts to escape the idea of marriage that Sterling and Sir John uphold, then we must also see in the play the rudiments of a world-view that would shake the security of Sterlings and Lord Oglebys to their very foundations.

Sources and Stage Histories

1. *The Clandestine Marriage*

The Clandestine Marriage was conceived from the start as a collaborative effort between the two dramatists, each of whom had been successful in their own right. George Colman was the more experienced writer; Garrick the more experienced man of the theatre. Colman had proven himself with such successes as *Polly Honeycombe* (1761) and *The Jealous Husband* (1763); Garrick's company had often demonstrated their accomplishments in stage comedy.

Henry William Pedicord and Frederick L. Bergmann have traced the genesis of the play fairly carefully in their edition of Garrick's plays (I, 413-20); only the outlines of the composition need be mentioned here. The initial idea for the play seems to have been Garrick's – a draft manuscript of a play entitled *The Sisters* sets out most of the action and characters of the completed play. Colman supplied names for Garrick's characters, suggested revisions to the draft, and worked out most of the business with characters who were to become Sterling and Mrs. Heidelberg. According to Pedicord and Bergmann, Colman was responsible chiefly for the Sir John Melvil scenes (about half of Act IV) and the scenes with the lawyers. Colman also wrote a version of Act V, but the version that was eventually produced is Garrick's, and the two collaborators seem to have ended their partnership – and, for a while, their friendship – over this last act.

However the two playwrights collaborated on the comedy as we have it, each was influenced by a variety of sources. Richard Bevis, working on suggestions from John Genest, sees the play as a re-working of *False Concord* (1764), an unpublished afterpiece by James Townley (*Laughing Tradition* 179-80). *The Clandestine Marriage* does share some features in common with Townley's play: in its social comedy it is clearly in the same spirit as much of Colman's work. The writers themselves list two older sources as their primary inspiration: William Hogarth's *Marriage a-la-Mode* (1745) and a satirical novel by John Shebbeare, *The Marriage Act* (1754). These sources offer more fruitful ground for exploring some of the main satirical themes of the play. Both sources satirise marriage; in particular, they attack contracted marriages devised by parents to turn the institution of marriage into a money-making scheme.

Hogarth's narrative traces the decline of the marriage of Lord Squanderfield and a merchant's daughter. The opening plate shows a lawyer arranging the marriage with the gouty Lord Squanderfield (father of the groom) and a London merchant (father of the bride). The bride and groom themselves are both present, but neither is paying much attention to the legal dealings: the younger Lord Squanderfield, in particular, is busy admiring himself in a mirror and taking snuff. Lord Squanderfield is clearly driven by financial considerations to make this match successful: one lawyer hands him a document labelled "Mortgage," while his other hands holds a cheque for £1000, perhaps taken from the pile of cash the merchant has just paid for the marriage. While the merchant pays careful attention to the terms of the settlement, Lord Squanderfield merely points to his family tree, as if to indicate that his name and title should be enough to offer in this marriage. The position of the couple in the whole affair is indicated by two pointers who are chained together in the bottom right corner of the picture. Hogarth's moral series ends tragically, with the death of the Count at the hands of the Countess's lover and the Countess's suicide, grief-stricken at her marital infidelity. The point is clear enough: fashionable marriage, unconcerned as it is with the true values of marriage, is doomed to end in tragedy.

The main plot of *The Marriage Act* shares much in common with Hogarth's series, and thus also resembles the general outline of *The Clandestine Marriage*. Barter and his wife roughly correspond to Sterling and Mrs. Heidelberg; Molly, the elder daughter, is a status-seeker like Betsey Sterling while Eliza Barter is in love with Barter's impoverished clerk, William Worthy. Lord Wormeaton roughly corresponds to Lord Ogleby while Wormeaton's son, Lord Sapplin, suggests Sir John Melvil. In fact, the name "Lord Sapplin" appears in one of the early drafts of the play as the name of the character who eventually appears as Sir John.

Shebbeare's novel is a direct response to Lord Hardwicke's Marriage Act of 1753, which reformed marriage laws instituted in Tudor times. Lawrence Stone has noted that the Act reduced the importance of the sacramental aspect of marriage, and did away with the notion that "marriage" could be understood as a private, verbal contract between the bride and groom. Prior to the Act, marriages were primarily canonical affairs, and were considered indissoluble. After 1753, the only unions recognised as "marriage" were those accompanied by legal, written contracts, signed in the presence of witnesses. In theory, a marriage could only be performed by a clergyman after the proper canonical banns had been published. In practice, clergymen were only too willing, for a fee, to waive the banns and perform the ceremony on demand. Parental interference was useless in such cases, and there was nothing to stop unscrupulous young men from seducing young women to get at their fathers' estates. In fact, then, the new Act did not do much to protect the interests of young women and their justifiably nervous fathers.

Shebbeare argues in *The Marriage Act* that the Act is no better than the laws it was intended to replace since the act denigrates a holy institution, presumably based on love, to an aspect of private life dominated by lawyers. One clause in particular states that no woman under the age of twenty-one may marry without her father's consent. However, the Act says nothing about fathers arranging marriages without their daughters' consent, and it is that disparity that Shebbeare attacks. By way of example the novel presents a wealthy merchant, Mr. Barter, who, like Garrick and Colman's Sterling, arranges for his eldest daughter to be married to an impoverished nobleman. The deal is contracted between the two men alone, to their mutual benefit: Barter, the merchant, raises his social status by marrying into a titled family; in return, the poor head of the titled family obtains badly-need capital. The daughter is thus little more than a commodity, her worth determined by her marketability to nobles. The novel builds on this basic plot with other stories about true lovers who have been separated because of the same clause, including a couple who resemble Fanny and Lovewell in the present play.

Garrick and Colman also explore some of the implications of the Marriage Act in their play, and, like Shebbeare, satirize the notion of marriage as a legal arrangement rather than a spiritual union between two souls. The "clandestine marriage" of the title presents complications which bar Sterling and Sir John Melvil from exchanging Betsey Sterling for Fanny. The play explicitly shows that Sterling thinks primarily in terms of business: his talk of family honour is revealed to be a facade when he realises he can save a significant amount of money from Sir John's desires:

SIR JOHN
Now if you will but consent to my waving that marriage –

STERLING
I agree to your waving that marriage? Impossible, Sir John!

SIR JOHN

I hope not, Sir; as on my part, I will agree to wave my
right to thirty thousand pounds of the fortune I was to receive with her.

STERLING

Thirty thousand, d'ye say?

SIR JOHN

Yes, Sir; and accept of Miss Fanny with fifty thousand, instead of fourscore.

STERLING

Fifty thousand – (*pausing.*)

SIR JOHN

Instead of fourscore.

STERLING

Why, – why, – there may be something in that...Why – to
do you justice, Sir John, there is something fair and open
in your proposal; and since I find you do not mean to put
an affront upon the family –

SIR JOHN

Nothing was ever farther from my thoughts, Mr. Sterling.
– And after all, the whole affair is nothing extraordinary –
such things happen every day – and as the world has only
heard generally of a treaty between the families, when this
marriage takes place, nobody will be the wiser, if we have
but discretion enough to keep our own counsel.

STERLING

True, true; and since you only transfer from one girl to the
other, it is no more than transferring so much stock, you
know.

SIR JOHN

The very thing. (III.i. 203-44)

Sterling's final line in the above passage is revealing: earlier he be-
rates Sir John by asking "Do you think that I drive a kind of African
slave trade with [my daughters]?"; by seeing them in terms of
"stock," however, he shows that the father who contracts marriage
deals without his daughter's knowledge or consent is, in fact, a kind
of slave-trader.

The Clandestine Marriage received its premiere at Drury Lane on
February 20, 1766. Curiously, it was initially performed without an

afterpiece: Garrick's Epilogue perhaps filled the role of short play after the mainpiece. It was an instant success, and was performed 18 times during the remainder of the 1765-66 season. Initial critical reaction was generally favourable, as the review in the *London Magazine* for February 1766 shows (see Appendix A). It soon appeared in print, although Francis Gentleman believed that the play worked better on the stage than in the closet. The play closed on May 15, 1766, perhaps because Thomas King, who created the part of Lord Ogleby, suffered a serious accident two days after this performance and was unable to return to the stage until the following season.

When the play was revived on October 17, 1766, it was invariably performed with an afterpiece. The first two were Isaac Bickerstaffe's *Daphne and Amintor* and James Love's *The Hermit* – incidentally, both pastoral pieces. The day after the premiere of *The Cunning-Man* on November 21, 1766, *The Clandestine Marriage* was performed with Burney's interlude. The night of December 3 particularly showcased the Burney family, as Charles Rousseau Burney (billed as "Mr. Burney jr. of Worcester"), Burney's nephew, premiered a new Harpsichord Concerto between the plays. During the 1766-67 season, *The Clandestine Marriage* was played 16 times, four times with Burney's afterpiece. This afterpiece was performed more than any other, with the exception of the Charles Burney/Henry Woodward collaboration, *Queen Mab* (1750), which was also performed four times.

The play's success, however, did not ensure a continuing collaboration between Garrick and Colman. Colman, upset both over Garrick's refusal to play Lord Ogleby in the premiere and over his rejection of Colman's final revisions for the play, left Drury Lane theatre altogether and became resident dramatist at Covent Garden. Later, Colman covertly claimed sole authorship of the play, a claim supported by his dramatist son, George Colman the Younger. Despite the rift, *The Clandestine Marriage* became part of the standard repertory at Drury Lane. It has even received modern revivals: in 1993 the University of Southern California mounted a student production and in 1994 Nigel Hawthorne directed a version of the play at London's Queen's Theatre (Hawthorne also starred as Lord Ogelby in the same production).

The Clandestine Marriage was popular in continental Europe as well, although not in its original form. In 1791, Domenico Cimarosa premiered *Il Matrimonio Segreto*, an operatic version of the comedy. Cimarosa's comic opera (*melodramme giocoso* in Italian) descends through an unusual line of transmission since his librettist, Giovanni Bertati, worked not from the Garrick and Colman original, but from a French version of the play that had been popular in the 1780s. Bertati significantly changes the focus of the story in order to transform a Drury Lane comedy into a comic opera for an Italian audience. The characters are no longer English, but Italian. Bertati also alters the setting, so that the entire action takes place in Sterling's (now Geronimo's) house, in various halls and rooms. He thus removes the satire on English landscape gardening, but in so doing also removes an important theme of the original play. Whereas *The Clandestine Marriage* is a comedy that contains pointed satirical barbs, *Il Matrimonio Segreto* is a charming love story about a secretly-married couple, the bride's bumbling mercantile father, and an eccentric English peer who resolves the plot.

2. The Cunning-Man

The theatrical and musical world of Georgian London was relatively small; it included a small coterie of artists who gathered frequently and, at least according to Boswell's *Life of Johnson*, determined the last word on all artistic matters. Charles Burney was part of this coterie, and he measured his success by his ability to retain his influential friendships. Like Johnson and Garrick, Burney was born outside of London, and was ambitious to make a name for himself in the capital. Unlike his counterparts, he had help from well-placed men: he was apprenticed to Thomas Arne, later chief composer at Drury Lane, and through Arne met Handel and became acquainted with the nobility. Burney was also patronised by an aristocrat, Fulke Greville, who acted partly as a musical patron and partly as an overseer to Burney's career. Margaret Anne Doody, in her biographical study of Frances Burney's writings, argues that Charles was obsessed with his social inferiority, and in part bullied his children to become successful as a way of proving himself.[6] Indeed, his children did distinguish themselves in music, literature, visual arts, and even in the navy. The frenetic pace of life in the Burney household is best seen in Frances's own early diaries. Garrick himself was a frequent visitor, and the Burney children grew up in a constant atmosphere of music and theatre.[7]

Burney composed very little original music: he was best known in his own time as a teacher, critic, and historian. His *Present State of Music in France and Italy* (1771) provides an invaluable record of performance practice in the late eighteenth century. That book, along with a six-volume *History of Music* published between 1776 and 1789, and a set of memoirs, heavily edited by Frances and published after her father's death, were Burney's major achievements.

During a tour of France in 1765 that provided much of the material for *The Present State of Music*, Burney heard a performance of Jean-Jacques Rousseau's *intermède, Le Devin du Village* (1752). Rousseau's play had been popular throughout Europe: even Louis XV – usually no great lover of music – had been heard humming its opening air. Burney prepared a translation of the libretto that could be sung to the original airs. At the same time, Garrick, who frequently tried to accustom English audiences to French tastes, had been considering introducing a version of *Le Devin* at Drury Lane as an alternative to Italian opera. He accepted Burney's version of the play, with some revisions, and *The Cunning-Man* was premiered November 21, 1766, as an afterpiece to Thomas Otway's *The Orphan*.

The timing of the afterpiece was auspicious. During 1766, Rousseau had been involved in a dispute with David Hume, after the former had sought political asylum in England. Rousseau claimed he had been ill-treated and ridiculed by Hume after accepting his initial offer. Hume denied the charges. This dispute heightened the public's appetite for Rousseau's writing, including his theatrical works.

Despite the unintentional publicity over the Hume-Rousseau affair – The *Gentleman's Magazine* ran a lengthy article in November 1766 that clearly defended Hume's position – both Burney and Garrick were anxious to make the play a success. Burney admits in his preface that he has abbreviated Rousseau's original second act to conform with the taste of the English stage:

> *Upon rehearsing the Music, it has been thought necessary to retrench the Second Act, for fear of satiety: for though the Airs and Dances, after the reconciliation of* Colin *and* Phoebe, *are by no means inferior to the rest in point of composition; yet, as no other business remained to be done after that circumstance but that of mere festivity, the Editor, with some reluctance, submitted to the omission of such*

*Airs, &c. as are printed with inverted commas: which, however, are
all published, with the Music, by Mr.* Bremner *in the* Strand.

The discrepancies between the version presented at Drury Lane and
the revised printed version (which the present text follows) show
that both Burney and Garrick kept their eyes carefully on the public
taste. In Burney's opinion, "mere festivity" would not be
enough to satisfy the patrons of Drury Lane; however, the airs
which constitute much of the music in Rousseau's second act
might be suitable for amateur or private presentations of Burney's
version of the piece.

Unfortunately, *The Cunning-Man* was not the success in England
that it was in the rest of Europe, although it received a respectable
fourteen performances in the 1766-67 season (see "Appendix A"
for a brief review from *The Gentleman's Magazine*). Percy Scholes
attributes the lacklustre reception of the piece to English taste: the
small cast and simple plot did not sit well with audiences used to
more lavish productions. However, *The Cunning-Man* can be considered Burney's most successful attempt at musical theatre. On the
strength of its success, Garrick invited him to compose music for
his burletta, *Orpheus*, which appeared as the rehearsal-piece in his
farce, *A Peep Behind the Curtain*. Garrick had also commissioned a
setting of the text from Barthélémon, who had composed the music
to the Epilogue of *The Clandestine Marriage*. Upon learning of the
rival setting, Burney refused to continue with his version, and indeed gave up writing music for the theatre altogether.

3. Bayes in Petticoats

As a contributing force to eighteenth-century dramatic writing,
women have been traditionally written out of the histories. Aphra
Behn was the most celebrated female dramatist but she is often
cited as an anomaly, an unusually outspoken woman whose deliberate flouting of convention is seen as much in the fact of her writing plays at all as in the plays she wrote. When women's contributions are spoken of at all, they are spoken of in terms of performance: the Restoration, after all, presented women on the stage in
England for the first time.

Of the performers, perhaps the most celebrated was Catherine
Clive – known by the more diminutive "Kitty" (a more fitting

name for a darling of the stage). Clive's biography, as interpreted by later stage historians such as Charles Lee Lewes, is a fantastic rags-to-riches story. It includes a tale of her discovery that is the eighteenth-century equivalent of the story of Lana Turner in Schwab's Pharmacy:

> When Mrs. Clive lived with Miss Knowles, who then lodged at Mrs. Snell's, a fan-painter in Church-Row, Houndsditch, Mr. Watson, many years box-keeper of Drury-Lane and Richmond, kept the Bell Tavern, directly opposite to Mrs. Snell's. At this house was held the Beef-Steak Club, instituted by Mr. Beard, Mr. Dunstall, Mr. Woodward, Stoppalaet, Bencraft, Giffard, &c.&c. Kitty Rafter, being one day washing the steps of the door, and singing, the windows of the club-room being open, they were instantly crowded by the company, who were all enchanted by her natural grace and simplicity. This circumstance alone led her to the stage, under the auspices of Mr. Beard and Mr. Dunstall (in Highfill, 3.342).

This story has by no means been verified, but it exemplifies the persona that Clive created: unassuming, full of "natural grace and simplicity." The anecdote mentions her singing talent; it does not mention her talent for comedy, which made her a central figure at Drury Lane in the years when stage comedy provided the most lucrative entertainment.

Clive also managed to maintain a public reputation as a respectable woman of the stage, in part because of her failed marriage. She had married George Clive, a lawyer, in 1733, but the marriage was over by 1734. Clive and her husband separated in 1735, but never divorced. Clive, therefore, could move freely among her male colleagues without scandal – in fact, her chastity became part of her endearing persona.

Bayes in Petticoats, the first of only two plays Clive composed, was written partly as a piece of self-parody. Clive had played the part of Buckingham's pompous poet in *The Rehearsal* (1671) – a satirical dig at John Dryden that became one of the most popular comedies of the 18th century – but by 1750 critics such as "Harry Rambler" were only too eager to point out that she was becoming too unattractive to play breeches parts. As a response, Clive created

Mrs. Hazard, the female counterpart to Buckingham's Bayes. Clive carries the parallel only so far: Mrs. Hazard begins as a comic figure, but ends up in a more sympathetic light than Buckingham's original.

In the original play, Bayes himself really is a bad playwright: overly conventional, and too proud of his own ideas to approach them critically. Buckingham's satire derives from Bayes's own pomposity – he cannot receive any constructive advice on how to improve his plays. At the opening of *Bayes in Petticoats*, we are tempted to see Mrs. Hazard the same way. Gatty, her maid, notes her ill-temper and Tom, her footman, mentions that she has become a laughing-stock because of her play:

> I fancy this Farce of her's is horrid Stuff: for I observe, all her Visitors she reads it to (which is indeed everybody that comes to the House) whisper as they come down Stairs, and laugh ready to kill themselves. (I.i. 15-18)

Indeed, when Mrs. Hazard first appears on stage, she is as nasty and ill-tempered as Gatty has described her. For the moment, Mrs. Hazard does resemble Bayes.

With the appearance of Witling, however, the perspective changes. Witling's name identifies him as a satirical figure; part of the foppish social circle that Mrs. Hazard moves in. Witling inadvertently reveals partly why Mrs. Hazard has become such a laughing-stock: no one expects to take seriously any play by a woman:

> I'll swear, [Witling reports himself saying] I believe Mrs. *Hazard* can write a very pretty Play, for she has a great deal of Wit and Humour. – Wit and Humour! says [Frank Surly], why there is not ten Women in Creation that have Sense enough to write a consistent N.B. (I.i. 84-86)

Frank Surly is not alone in his belief; the group of witlings who interrupt Mrs. Hazard's rehearsal refuse to take seriously any of the stage business.

Mrs. Hazard's attackers are of different types. The three women who show up at the theatre – Miss Giggle, Miss Sidle, and Miss Dawdle – are women who care for nothing but gossip and fashion. Mrs. Hazard is rightly outraged that Miss Giggle would use the theatre as a drawing-room; Witling himself remarks that he has brought this party to the theatre precisely to be revenged on Mrs. Hazard for making him "sick to death with her Stuff." The most condescending remarks, however, come from Sir Albany Odelove, an old rake who offers his advice on how to write plays:

> I say, Madam, will you give me leave, as you're going to en-
> tertain the Town, (that is, I mean, to endeavour, or to at-
> tempt to entertain them) for let me tell you, fair Lady, 'tis not
> an easy thing to bring about. If Men, who are properly
> graduated in Learning, who have swallow'd the Tincture of a
> polite Education, who, as I may say, are hand and glove with
> the Classics, if such Geniuses as I'm describing, fail of Success
> in Dramatical Occurrences, or Performances, ('tis the same
> Sense in the Latin) what must a poor Lady to expect, who is
> ignorant as the Dirt. (II.i. 258-67)

Mrs. Hazard, rightly furious, suspends her rehearsal shortly after-ward, and stomps off the stage. Witling, unfazed by the outburst, calls for a dance, and on that note the play ends.

The brutality of the witlings' behaviour in Act II marks them, and not Mrs. Hazard herself, as the objects of satire here. In Buck-ingham's play we clearly sympathise with the wits who ridicule Bayes, mainly because Bayes himself is so unaware that he is being ridiculed. Clive's play keenly portrays the frustration felt by a woman who wants to be taken seriously as a writer. Ironically, Mrs. Hazard's burletta (a portion of which is sung in Act II) is no worse than *The Cunning-Man* and, indeed, is in the same pastoral tradition as *Le Devin du village*. In *The Rehearsal*, the wits make fun of Bayes's play while it is being rehearsed, and in that play the genre of heroic drama as defined by Dryden is as much satirized as the playwright himself. Clive simply presents the text of her burletta without com-ment – the witlings arrive only after we have heard most of the text. Furthermore, there is nothing to indicate that the burletta is played farcically: Mrs. Hazard herself sings the part of Marcella, as a stand-in for Clive, who has decided to skip the rehearsal.

Clive satirises herself as a performer, she satirises foppish London society, and she satirises attitudes towards women writers that she no doubt knew herself, but she does not satirise Mrs. Hazard. She is far too wronged in Act II for the reader to see her as an object of ridicule. *Bayes in Petticoats* is a dark farce, a comedy which questions the notion of public taste, and the gender discrimination which receives fuller treatment in Frances Brooke's novel, *The Excursion* (1778). Unfortunately, the witlings triumph: Mrs. Hazard suggests that she is "not sure that [she] will ever have another" rehearsal, and she tears her manuscript to pieces as she leaves the stage. Witling laconically comments that "her tearing it, will only save the Audience the Trouble of doing it for her." In that he misses the point: no one has attacked the play itself, and Mrs. Hazard's great frustration lies in her being questioned that, as a woman, she is capable of writing one at all.

Bayes in Petticoats premiered March 15, 1750, at a benefit night for Clive. The mainpiece was *Hamlet*; Clive performed Ophelia. Prompter Richard Cross, who plays himself in the farce, notes that the play was well-received, and it was performed five more times during the 1749-50 season. After that, the play remained unperformed until March 10, 1753 – when Clive presented a revised version of the second act. That version was subsequently published and has formed the basis of the present text. On April 3 the piece was performed "by desire," but by October 31 the public seems to have grown tired of it: Cross notes that it was "hiss'd a little." Its final performance during Garrick's tenure was March 22, 1762, again at a benefit night for Clive, when it was presented with further alterations to the burletta portion. The text of those alterations has not survived.

Notes

1.   For example, in November 1755, Garrick featured as an afterpiece *The Chinese Festival*, a ballet by the French dance troupe of Georges St-Jean Noverre. Garrick was not prepared for the heated battle between pro-French and anti-French factions that swept through the house. Riots ensued almost every night that the *Festival* was mounted. On November 18, a fight spilled into the streets and prompted a reading of the Riot Act. Some of the rioters proceeded to Garrick's house in nearby Southampton St. and smashed his windows.

2.   Shakespeare and Jonson were always popular, and many Restoration standards, such as *The Country Wife* (1675), *The Man*

of *Mode* (1676), *Venice Preserv'd* (1682), *Love for Love* (1695) and *The Way of the World* (1700), continued to draw audiences. Susannah Centlivre's *The Busy Body* (1709) and *The Wonder* (1714) were, according to Bevis, two of four "non-Shakespearean comedies written before 1750" still in repertory in 1900 (*Laughing Tradition* 8). *The Beggar's Opera* (1728) was also performed innumerable times throughout the period.

3. The public tenaciously guarded other privileges as well. For example, in February 1763 Covent Garden mounted a lavish, expensive production of Thomas Arne's opera *Artaxerxes*. To defray the production costs, the management cancelled the half-price privilege. A riot ensued during the performance, described in the *Gentleman's Magazine*:

> All the benches of the boxes and Pit [were] entirely tore up, the glasses and chandeliers broken, and the linings of the boxes cut to pieces. The rashness of the rioters was so great, that they cut away the the wooden pillars between the boxes, so that if the inside of them had not been made of iron, they would have brought down the Galleries on their heads. The damages done amount to at least l2000.

4. There is no evidence that Swift's suggestion that Gay write "a Newgate pastoral" was, in fact, Gay's inspiration for *The Beggar's Opera*. The play is more overtly a satire on operatic conventions than on pastoral *per se*, but the scenes with Lucy Lockit in Act II, particularly the closing song ("I like the fox shall grieve"), directly draw from the pastoral tradition, and are therefore parodied when set in the context of Newgate prison.

5. Pope's "Discourse on Pastoral Poetry," for example, argues that the poetry of rustics is useful primarily for "giving us an esteem for the virtues of a former age." Rustic verse, he argues, being historically closest to the Golden Age of any poetry, must preserve more of the Golden Age than any other poetry.

6. Doody points specifically to Charles Burney's insistence that Frances accept the post of Second Keeper of the Robes to

Queen Charlotte in 1786, even though the ritual, seclusion and *ennui* of court life proved unbearable for the successful novelist. Burney saw his daughter's presence at court as a way of attaining royal influence.

7. Frances Burney makes frequent reference in her early diary to *The Clandestine Marriage*; Lord Ogleby was clearly one of her favourite characters (*Early Journals and Letters* I, 94; II, 137).

Bibliography

Alpers, Paul. "What is Pastoral?" *Critical Inquiry* 8 (3) Spring 1982.

Austen, Jane. *Pride and Prejudice.* 1813. Ed. James Kinsley and Frank W. Bradbrook. Oxford World's Classics ser. Oxford: Oxford UP, 1970.

Benjamin, Lewis E. *Stage Favourites of the Eighteenth Century.* 1928. Freeport, N.Y.: Books for Libraries P, 1969.

Berger, John. *Ways of Seeing: A Book.* London: BBC, 1972.

Bermingham, Ann. *Landscape and Ideology: The English Rustic Tradition 1740-1860255D. Berkeley: U of California P, 1986.*

Bevis, Richard W. The Laughing Tradition: Stage Comedy in Garrick's Day. Athens, U of Georgia P, 1980.

Bevis, Richard W., ed. *Eighteenth Century Drama: Afterpieces.* Oxford: Oxford UP, 1970.

Buckingham, George Villiars, Duke of. *The Rehearsal.* 1671. *Burlesque Plays of the Eighteenth Century.* Ed. Simon Trussler. Oxford: Oxford UP, 1969.

Burney, Frances. *Early Letters and Journals.* Ed. Lars E. Troide. 2 vols. Montreal and Kingston: McGill-Queen's UP, 1990-91.

Cimarosa, Domenico. *Il Matrimonio Segreto.* 1791. With Ryland Davies, Dietrich Fischer-Dieskau, and Arléen Auger. English Chamber Orchestra, cond. Daniel Barenboim. Deutsche Grammophon CD 437 696-2.

Dircks, Phyllis T. "Garrick's Fail-Safe Musical Venture, 'A Peep Behind the Curtain,' an English Burletta." *The Stage and the Page* 136-147.

Doody, Margaret Anne. *Frances Burney: The Life in the Works.* New Brunswick, NJ: Rutgers UP, 1988.

Empson, William. *Some Versions of Pastoral.* London: Oxford UP, 1935.

Ettin, Andrew V. *Literature and the Pastoral.* New Haven: Yale UP, 1984.

Gay, John. *The Beggar's Opera. The Dramatic Works.* 2 vols. Ed. John Fuller. Oxford: Clarendon, 1983.

Genest, John. *Some Account of the English Stage, From the Restoration in 1660 to 1830255D. 10 vols. 1832.* New York: Burt Franklin, 1965.

George, M. Dorothy. London Life in the Eighteenth Century. rev. ed. London: Penguin, 1951.

Hardin, Richard, ed. *Survivals of Pastoral.* Lawrence: U of Kansas P, 1979.

Heartz, Daniel. "The Beginnings of the Operatic Romance: Rousseau, Sedaine, and Monsigny." *Eighteenth-Century Studies* 15.2 (Winter 1981-82): 149-178.

Highfill, Phillip, ed. *A Biographical Dictionary of Actors, Actresses, Musicians, Dancers, Managers, and other Stage Personnel in London, 1660-1800255D. 16 vols.* Carbondale, Southern Illinois UP, 1973- .

Hogarth, William. Hogarth's Graphic Works. 3rd. ed. Ed. Ronald Paulson. London: The Print Room, 1989.

Hughes, Leo. "A Flawed Tribute to Garrick." *Modern Philology* 80.4 (May 1983): 398-405.

Lonsdale, Roger. *Dr. Charles Burney. A Literary Biography.* Oxford: Clarendon, 1965.

Malins, Edward. *English Landscaping and Literature 1660-1840255D.* London: Oxford UP, 1966.

Murphy, Arthur. The Life of Garrick. 2 vols. London, 1801.

Pedicord, Harry William. *The Theatrical Public in the Time of Garrick.* Carbondale: Southern Illinois UP, 1956.

——. "On-Stage with David Garrick: Garrick's Acting Companies in Peformance." *Theatre Survey* 28.2 (November 1977): 51-74.

Pedicord, Harry William and Frederick L. Bergmann, eds. *The Dramatic Works of David Garrick.* 6 vols. Carbondale: Southern Illinois UP. 1982.

Porter, Roy. *English Society in the Eighteenth Century.* rev. ed. The Penguin Social History of Britain ser. London: Penguin, 1990.

Rebejkow, Jean-Christophe. "Sur *Le Devin du Village* de Jean-Jacques Rousseau et ses relectures par Diderot." *Francofonia* 20 (Spring 1991): 61-74.

Rizzo, Betty. "How (and How Not) to Explore the Burneys: Questions of Decorum." *Review* 11 (1989): 197-218.

Rousseau, Jean-Jacques. *Le Devin de Village.* 1752. With Eva Kirshner. Alpe Adria Ensemble, cond. René Clemencic. Nouveau Era Nov-7106.

Scholes, Percy A. *The Great Dr. Burney.* 2 vols. London: Oxford UP, 1948.

Scholes, Percy A. and Watkins Shaw. "Charles Burney." *The New Grove Dictionary of Music and Musicians.*

Shebbeare, John. *The Marriage Act.* London, 1754.

Stewart, Stanley. *The Enclosed Garden*. Madison: U of Wisconsin P, 1966.

Stone, George Winchester, Jr. and George M. Kahrl. *David Garrick. A Critical Biography*. Carbondale: Southern Illinois UP, 1979.

Stone, George Winchester, Jr., ed. *The London Stage 1660-1800. Part 4: 1747-1776255D. 3 vols. Carbondale: Southern Illinois UP, 1962.

——, ed. The Stage and the Page: London's "Whole Show" in *Eighteenth-Century Theatre*. Berkeley: U of California P, 1987.

"Sylvanus Urban," ed. *The Gentleman's Magazine*. Vol. 36. London, 1766.

Tate Gallery. *Manners and Morals: Hogarth and British Painting 1700-1760255D. London: Tate Gallery, 1987.

Tierney, James E. "Recent Studies in Eighteenth-Century Drama." *Philological Quarterly* 62.3 (Summer 1983): 335-352.

Vance, John A. "A Peep Behind the Curtain: David Garrick, Playwright and Adaptor." *Papers on Language and Literature* 20.3 (Summer 1984): 339-351.

Voisine, Jacques. "*Le Devin du Village* de Jean-Jacques Rousseau et son adaptation anglaise par le musicologue Charles Burney." *Le Theatre dans l'Europe des Lumières: Programmes, practiques, échanges*. Ed. Mieczyslaw Klimowicz and Aleksander Labuda. Warsaw: Wydawnitcwo Uniwersytetu Wrocawskiego, 1985, 133-146.

THE

Clandeſtine Marriage,

A

C O M E D Y.

As it is ACTED at the

Theatre-Royal in *Drury-Lane.*

BY

G E O R G E   C O L M A N

AND

D A V I D   G A R R I C K.

Huc adhibe vultus, et in unâ parce duobus :
Vivat, et ejuſdem ſimus uterque parens !   OVID.

L O N D O N:

Printed for T. BECKET and P. A. DE HONDT, in the Strand ;
R. BALDWIN, in Pater-noſter-Row ; R. DAVIS, in Pic-
cadilly ; and T. DAVIES, in Ruſſel-Street, Covent-
Garden.

M.DCC.LXVI.

Ovid] *Amores* 2.13. 15-16, altered.

ADVERTISEMENT

Hogarth's MARRIAGE-A-LA-MODE has before furnished Materials to the Author of a Novel, published some Years ago, under the title of *The Marriage-Act*. But as that Writer pursued a very different Story, and as his Work was chiefly designed for a Political Satire, very little Use could be made of it for the Service of this Comedy. In Justice to the Person, who has been considered as the sole   5 Author, the Party, who has hitherto lain concealed, thinks it incumbent on him to declare, that the Disclosure of his Name was, by his own Desire, reserved till the Publication of the Piece.

Both the Authors, however, who have before been separately honoured with the Indulgence of the Publick, now beg Leave to   10 make their joint Acknowledgements for the very favourable Reception of the CLANDESTINE MARRIAGE.

---

1 MARRIAGE-A-LA-MODE] See "Introduction," (pp. *xxv–xxvi*), for a discussion of Hogarth's influence on the play.

2 *The Marriage-Act*] By John Shebbeare, published 1754. Garrick and Colman used this novel as a source for the plot and themes of *The Clandestine Marriage*. See "Introduction," pp. *xxvi–xxvii*

5-6 sole Author] George Colman. But see "Introduction," pp. *xxiv–xxv*, *xxviii–xxix* and "Textual Note".

PROLOGUE.

Written by Mr. Garrick.
Spoken by Mr. Holland.

Poets and Painters, who from Nature draw
Their best and richest Stores, have made this Law:
That each should neighbourly assist his Brother,
And steal with Decency from one another.
Tonight, your matchless Hogarth gives the Thought,   5
Which from his Canvas to the Stage is brought.
And who so fit to warm the Poet's mind,
As he who pictur'd Morals and Mankind?
But not the same their Characters and Scenes;
Both labour for one End, by different Means: 10
Each, as it suits him, takes a separate Road,
Their one great Object, MARRIAGE-A-LA-MODE!
Where Titles deign with Cits to have and hold,
And change rich Blood for more substantial Gold!
And honour'd Trade from Interest turns aside,   15
To hazard Happiness for titled Pride.
The Painter dead, yet still he charms the Eye;
While England lives, his Fame can never die:
But he who struts his Hour upon the Stage
Can scarce extend his Fame for Half an Age;   20
Nor Pen nor Pencil can the Actor save,
The Art, and Artist, share one common Grave.

3-4 *That each...from one another*] Perhaps an allusion to Peachum's opening song
(Air I) in *The Beggar's Opera*:

> Through all the Employments of Life
> Each Neighbour abuses his Brother;
> Whore and Rogue they call Husband and Wife
> All Professions be-rogue one another.

13 *Titles...Cits*] "Titles" are the landed gentry; "cits" are "inhabitant[s] of a city,
in an ill sense. Pert, low, townsm[e]n; pragmatical trader[s]" (Johnson). This
and the subsequent line allude to one of the main satiric barbs of the play, that
of Lord Ogleby's willingness to marry beneath his class out of need for
Sterling's money.

19 struts..the Stage] *Macbeth* 5.5.25.

Oh, let me drop one tributary Tear
On poor Jack Falstaff's Grave, and Juliet's Bier!
You to their Worth must Testimony give; 25
'Tis in your Hearts alone their Fame can live.
Still as the Scenes of Life will shift away,
The strong Impressions of their Art decay.
Your Children cannot feel what you have known;
They'll boast of QUINS *and* CIBBERS *of their own:* 30
The greatest Glory of our happy few
Is to be felt, and be approv'd by YOU.

---

24 Jack Falstaff...Juliet] Shakespearean roles for which James Quin and Susannah
Cibber were best known. See following note.

30 QUINS *and* CIBBERS] An allusion to the recent deaths of James Quin and
Susannah Cibber. Arthur Murphy notes that Cibber died 30 January 1766 and
Quin in March of the same year. He remarks that "Garrick spoke a most
handsome funeral elogium on [Quin] and Mrs. Cibber, at the close of his
prologue to the *Clandestine Marriage*" (*Life* II.36). This allusion suggests that
this Prologue was not spoken at the play's première, or was revised for
publication to include the elegy on Quin.

DRAMATIS PERSONÆ

MEN

Lord Ogleby	Mr. KING
Sir John Melvil	Mr. HOLLAND
Sterling	Mr. YATES
Lovewell	Mr. POWELL
Canton	Mr. BADDELEY
Brush	Mr. PALMER
Serjeant Flower	Mr. LOVE
Traverse	Mr. LEE
Trueman	Mr. AICKIN

WOMEN

Mrs. Heidelberg	Mrs. CLIVE
Miss Sterling	Miss POPE
Fanny	Mrs. PALMER
Betty	Mrs. [ABINGTON]
Chambermaid	Miss PLYM
Trusty	Miss MILLS

THE

CLANDESTINE MARRIAGE

SCENE, *A room in Sterling's house.*
Miss Fanny *and* Betty *meeting.*

BETTY [*Running in*].

Ma'am! Miss Fanny! Ma'am!

FANNY.

What's the matter! Betty!

BETTY.

Oh la! Ma'am! As sure as I'm alive, here is your husband –

FANNY.

Hush! My dear Betty! If anybody in the house should hear
you, I am ruined.   5

BETTY.

Mercy on me! it has frighted me to such a degree, that my
heart is come up to my mouth. – But as I was saying, Ma'am,
here's that dear, sweet –

FANNY.

Have a care! Betty.

BETTY.

Lord! I'm bewitched, I think. – But as I was a saying, Ma'am,   10
here's Mr. Lovewell just come from London.

FANNY.

Indeed!

BETTY.

Yes, indeed, and indeed, Ma'am, he is. I saw him crossing the
court-yard in his boots.

FANNY.

I am glad to hear it. – But pray now, my dear Betty, be cau-   15
tious. Don't mention that word again, on any account. You
know, we have agreed never to drop any expressions of that
sort for fear of an accident.

BETTY.

> Dear Ma'am, you may depend on me. There is not a more
> trustier creature on the face of the earth, than I am. Though I   20
> say it, I am as secret as the grave – and if it's never told, till I
> tell it, it may remain untold till doom's-day for Betty.

FANNY.

> I know you are faithful – but in our circumstances we cannot
> be too careful.

BETTY.

> Very true, Ma'am! – and yet I vow and protest, there's more   25
> plague than pleasure with a secret; especially if a body mayn't
> mention it to four or five of one's particular acquaintance.

FANNY.

> Do but keep this secret a little while longer, and then, I hope
> you may mention it to any body. – Mr. Lovewell will ac-
> quaint the family with the nature of our situation as soon as   30
> possible.

BETTY.

> The sooner, the better, I believe. For if he does not tell it,
> there'a a little tell-tale, I know of, will come and tell it for
> him.

FANNY   [*Blushing*].

> Fie, Betty!   35

BETTY.

> Ah, you may well blush. – But you're not so sick, and so pale,
> and so wan, and so many qualms –

FANNY.

> Have done! I shall be quite angry with you.

BETTY.

> Angry! – Bless the dear puppet! I am sure I shall love it as
> much as if it was my own. – I meant no harm, heaven knows.   40

FANNY.

> Well – say no more of this. – It makes me uneasy. All I have to
> ask of you is to be faithful and secret, and not to reveal this
> matter, till we disclose it to the family ourselves.

BETTY.

> Me reveal it! – if I say a word, I wish I may be burned. I
> would not do you any harm for the world. – And as for Mr.   45
> Lovewell, I am sure I have loved the gentleman ever since he

got a tide-waiter's place for my brother. – But let me tell you both, you must leave off your soft looks to each other, and your whispers, and your glances, and your always sitting next to one another at dinner, and your long walks together in the evening. – For my part, if I had not been in the secret, I should have known you were a pair of loviers at least, if not man and wife, as –

FANNY.

See there now! again. Pray be careful.

BETTY.

Well – well – nobody hears me. – Man and wife – I'll say so no more – what I tell you is very true, for all that –

LOVEWELL [Calling within].

William!

BETTY.

Hark! I hear your husband –

FANNY.

What!

BETTY.

I say, here comes Mr. Lovewell. – Mind the caution I give you. – I'll be whipped now if you are not the first person he sees or speaks to in the family. – However, if you chuse it, it's nothing at all to me – as you sow, you must reap – as you brew, so you must bake. – I'll e'en slip down the back stairs and leave you two together.

Exit.

FANNY [Alone].

I see, I see I shall never have a moment's ease till our marriage is made publick. New distresses croud in upon me every day. The sollicitude of my mind sinks my spirits, preys upon my health, and destroys every comfort of my life. It shall be revealed, let what will be the consequence.

---

46 tide-waiter] "An officer who watches the lading of goods at the customhouse" (Johnson).

Enter Lovewell.

LOVEWELL.

My love! – How's this? – In tears? – Indeed this is too much. You promised me to support your spirits, and to wait the determination of our fortune with patience. – For my sake, for your own, be comforted! Why will you study to add to our 75 uneasiness and perplexity?

FANNY.

Oh, Mr. Lovewell! The indelicacy of a secret marriage grows every day more and more shocking to me. I walk about the house like a guilty wretch: I imagine myself the object of suspicion of the whole family; and am under the perpetual ter- 80 rors of a shameful detection.

LOVEWELL.

Indeed, indeed, you are to blame. The amiable delicacy of your temper, and your quick sensibility, only serve to make you unhappy. – To clear up this affair properly to Mr. Sterling, is the continual employment of my thoughts. Every thing now is in a fair train. It begins to grow ripe for a discovery; 85 and I have no doubt of its concluding to the satisfaction of ourselves, of your father, and the whole family.

FANNY.

End how it will, I am resolved it shall end soon – very soon. – I would not live another week in this agony of mind to be mistress of the universe. 90

LOVEWELL.

Do not be too violent neither. Do not let us disturb the joy of your sister's marriage with the tumult this matter may occasion! – I have brought letters from Lord Ogleby and Sir John Melvil to Mr. Sterling. – They will be here this evening – and, I dare say, within this hour. 95

FANNY.

I am sorry for it.

LOVEWELL.

Why so?

FANNY.

No matter. – Only let us disclose our marriage immediately!

LOVEWELL.

As soon as possible.

FANNY.

But directly. 100

LOVEWELL.

In a few days, you may depend on it.

FANNY.

Tonight – or tomorrow morning.

LOVEWELL.

That, I fear, will be impracticable.

FANNY.

Nay, but you must.

LOVEWELL.

Must! why? 105

FANNY.

Indeed, you must. – I have the most alarming reasons for it.

LOVEWELL.

Alarming, indeed! For they alarm me, even before I am acquainted with them. – What are they?

FANNY.

I cannot tell you.

LOVEWELL.

Not tell me? 110

FANNY.

Not at present. When all is settled, you shall be acquainted
with every thing.

LOVEWELL.

Sorry they are coming! – Must be discovered! – What can
this mean! – Is it possible you can have any reasons that need
be concealed from me? 115

FANNY.

Do not disturb yourself with conjectures – but rest assured,
that though you are unable to divine the cause, the consequence of a discovery, be it what it will, cannot be attended
with half the miseries of the present interval.

LOVEWELL.

You put me upon the rack. – I would do any thing to make 120
you easy. – But you know your father's temper. – Money
(you will excuse my frankness) is the spring of all his actions,
which nothing but the idea of acquiring nobility or magnifi-
cence can ever make him forego – and these he thinks
money will purchase. – You know too your aunt's, Mrs. 125

Heidelberg's, notions of the splendour of high life, her contempt for everything that does not relish of what she calls Quality, and that from the vast fortune in her hands, by her late husband, she absolutely governs Mr. Sterling and the whole family: now, if they should come to the knowledge of this affair too abruptly, they might, perhaps, be incensed beyond all hopes of reconciliation. 130

FANNY.

But if they are made acquainted with it otherwise than by ourselves, it will be ten times worse: and a discovery grows every day more probable. The whole family have long suspected our affection. We are also in the power of a foolish maid-servant; and if we may even depend on her fidelity, we cannot answer for her discretion. – Discover it therefore immediately, lest some accident should bring it to light, and involve us in additional disgrace. 135 140

LOVEWELL.

Well – well – I meant to discover it soon but would not do it too precipitately. – I have more than once sounded Mr. Sterling about it, and will attempt him more seriously the next opportunity. But my principal hopes are these. – My relationship to Lord Ogleby, and his having placed me with your father, have been, you know, the first links in the chain of this connection between the two families; in consequence of which, I am at present in high favour with all parties: while they all remain thus well-affected to me, I propose to lay our case before the old Lord; and if I can prevail on him to mediate in this affair, I make no doubt but he will be able to appease your father; and, being a lord and a man of quality, I am sure he may bring Mrs. Heidelberg into good-humour at any time. – Let me beg you, therefore, to have but a little patience, as, you see, we are upon the very eve of a discovery, that must probably be to our advantage. 145 150 155

FANNY.

Manage it in your own way. I am persuaded.

LOVEWELL.

But in the meantime make yourself easy.

FANNY.

As easy as I can, I will. – We had better not remain together any longer at present. – Think of this business, and let me know how you proceed.　160

LOVEWELL.

Depend on my care! But, pray, be chearful.

FANNY.

I will.

As she is going out, enter Sterling.

STERLING.

Hey-day! Who have we got here?

FANNY [*Confused*].

Mr. Lovewell, Sir!　165

STERLING.

And where are you going, hussey!

FANNY.

To my sister's chamber, Sir!

Exit.

STERLING.

Ah, Lovewell! What! always getting my foolish girl yonder into a corner! – Well – well – let us but once see her elder sister fast-married to Sir John Melvil, we'll soon provide a good husband for Fanny, I warrant you.　170

LOVEWELL.

Would to heaven, Sir, you would provide her one of my recommendation!

STERLING.

Yourself? eh, Lovewell!

LOVEWELL.

With your pleasure, Sir!　175

STERLING.

Mighty well!

LOVEWELL.

And I flatter myself, that such a proposal would not be disagreeable to Miss Fanny.

STERLING.

Better and better!

LOVEWELL.

And if I could but obtain your consent, Sir –   180

STERLING.

What! You marry Fanny! – No – no – that will never do,
Lovewell! – You're a good boy, to be sure – I have a great
value for you – but can't think of you for a son-in-law. –
There's no *Stuff* in the case, no money, Lovewell!

LOVEWELL.

My pretensions to fortune, indeed, are but moderate, but   185
though not equal to splendour, sufficient to keep us above
distress. – Add to which, that I hope by diligence to increase
it – and have love, honour –

STERLING.

But not the *Stuff*, Lovewell! – Add one little round o to the
sum total of your fortune, and that will be the finest thing   190
you can say to me. – You know I've a regard for you – would
do any thing to serve you – any thing on the footing of
friendship – but –

LOVEWELL.

If you think me worthy of your friendship, Sir, be assured that
there is no instance in which I should rate your friendship so 195
highly.

STERLING.

Psha! psha! that's another thing, you know. – Where money or
interest is concerned, friendship is quite out of the question.

LOVEWELL.

But where the happiness of a daughter is at stake, you would
not scruple, sure, to sacrifice a little to her inclinations.   200

STERLING.

Inclinations! Why, you would not persuade me that the girl is
in love with you – eh, Lovewell!

LOVEWELL.

I cannot absolutely answer for Miss Fanny, Sir; but am sure
that the chief happiness or misery of my life depends entirely
upon her.   205

STERLING.

Why, indeed now if your kinsman, Lord Ogleby, would come
down handsomely for you – but that's impossible. – No, no –

'twill never do – I must hear no more of this. – Come, Lovewell, promise me that I shall hear no more of this.

LOVEWELL [*Hesitating*].

I am afraid, Sir, I should not be able to keep my word with 210
you, if I did promise you.

STERLING.

Why, you would not offer to marry her without my consent? would you, Lovewell!

LOVEWELL [*Confused*].

Marry her, Sir!

STERLING.

Ay, marry her, Sir! – I know very well that a warm speech or 215
two from such a dangerous young spark, as you are, will go
much farther towards persuading a silly girl to do what she
has more than a month's mind to do, than twenty grave lec-
tures from fathers or mothers, or uncles or aunts, to prevent
her. – But you would not, sure, be such a base fellow, such a 220
treacherous young rogue, as to seduce my daughter's affections, and destroy the peace of my family in that manner. – I
must insist on it, that you give me your word not to marry
her without my consent.

LOVEWELL.

Sir – I – I – as to that – I – I – I – beg, Sir. – Pray, Sir, excuse 225
me on this subject at present.

STERLING.

Promise, then, that you will carry this matter no further
without my approbation.

LOVEWELL.

You may depend on it, Sir, that it shall go no further.

STERLING.

Well – well – that's enough – I'll take care of the rest, I war- 230
rant you. – Come, come, let's have done with this nonsense! –
What's doing in town? – Any news upon 'Change?

---

232 'Change] The Royal Exchange, situated on Threadneedle Street, hence in
the heart of mercantile London. Sterling is particularly concerned here about
news from his foreign investments.

LOVEWELL.

Nothing material.

STERLING.

Have you seen the currants, the soap, and Madeira, safe in the warehouses? Have you compared the goods with the invoice   235
and bills of lading, and are they all right?

LOVEWELL.

They are, Sir!

STERLING.

And how are stocks?

LOVEWELL.

Fell one and an half this morning.

STERLING.

Well – well – some good news from America and they'll be   240
up again. – But how are Lord Ogleby and Sir John Melvil?
When are we to expect them?

LOVEWELL.

Very soon, Sir! I came on purpose to bring you their commands. Here are letters from both of them. [*Giving letters.*]

STERLING.

Let me see – let me see – 'Slife, how his Lordship's letter is   245
perfumed! – It takes my breath away – [*Opening it.*] And
French paper, too! With a fine border of flowers and flour-
ishes – and a slippery gloss on it that dazzles one's eyes. –
[*Reading.*] *My dear Mr. Sterling.* – Mercy on me, his Lordship
writes a worse hand than a boy at his exercise – But how's   250
this? Eh! – [*Reading.*] – *with you tonight* – *Lawyers tomorrow
morning.* Tonight! – that's sudden indeed. – Where's my sister
Heidelberg? she should know of this immediately. – [*Calling
the servants.*] Here John! Harry! Thomas! Hark ye, Lovewell!

LOVEWELL.

Sir!   255

STERLING.

Mind now, how I'll entertain his Lordship and Sir John. –
We'll shew your fellows at the other end of the town how we
live in the city. – They shall eat gold – and drink gold – and

---

245 'Slife] Contraction for "God's life"; a mild oath.

lie in gold. [*Calling.*] Here cook! Butler! What signifies your
birth and education, and titles? Money, money, that's the stuff   260
that makes the great man in this country.

LOVEWELL.

Very true, Sir!

STERLING.

True, Sir? – Why then, have done with your nonsense of love
and matrimony. You're not rich enough to think of a wife yet.
A man of business should mind nothing but his business. –   265
Where are these fellows? [*Calling.*] John! Thomas! – Get an
estate, and a wife will follow of course. – Ah! Lovewell! an
English merchant is the most respectable character in the
universe. 'Slife, man, a rich English merchant may make himself a match for the daughter of a Nabob. – Where are all my   270
rascals? Here, William!

Exit, calling.

LOVEWELL.

So! – As I suspected. – Quite averse to the match, and likely
to receive the news of it with great displeasure. – What's best
to be done? – Let me see! – Suppose I get Sir John Melvil to
interest himself in this affair. He may mention it to Lord   275
Ogleby with a better grace than I can, and more probably
prevail upon him to interfere in it. I can open my mind also
more freely to Sir John. He told me, when I left him in town,
that he had something of consequence to communicate, and
that I could be of use to him. I am glad of it: for the confi-   280
dence he reposes in me and the service I may do him will ensure me his good offices. – Poor Fanny! It hurts me to see her
so uneasy, and her making a mystery of the cause adds to my
anxiety. – Something must be done upon her account; for at
all events her sollicitude shall be removed.   285

Exit.

---

270 Nabob] An English merchant who has amassed great fortune in India.

SCENE *changes to another chamber.*

Enter Miss Sterling, *and* Miss Fanny.

MISS STERLING.

Oh, my dear sister, say no more! This is downright hypocrisy.
– You shall never convince me that you don't envy me beyond measure. – Well, after all, it is extremely natural. – It is
impossible to be angry with you.

FANNY.

Indeed, sister, you have no cause.   5

MISS STERLING.

And you really pretend not to envy me?

FANNY.

Not in the least.

MISS STERLING.

And you don't in the least wish that you was just in my situation?

FANNY.

No, indeed, I don't. Why should I?   10

MISS STERLING.

Why should you? – What! on the brink of marriage, fortune,
title. – But I had forgot. – There's that dear sweet creature Mr.
Lovewell in the case. – You would not break your faith with
your true love now for the world, I warrant you.

FANNY.

Mr. Lovewell! – always Mr. Lovewell! – Lord, what signifies   15
Mr. Lovewell, Sister?

MISS STERLING.

Pretty peevish soul! – Oh, my dear, grave, romantick sister! –
A perfect philosopher in petticoats! – Love and a cottage! –
Eh, Fanny! – Ah, give me indifference and a coach and six!

FANNY.

And why not the coach and six without the indifference? –   20
But, pray, when is this happy marriage of your's to be celebrated? – I long to give you joy.

MISS STERLING.

In a day or two – I can't tell exactly. – Oh, my dear sister –
[*Aside.*] I must mortify her a little. – I know you have a pretty

taste. Pray give me your opinion of my jewels. – How d'ye   25
like the stile of this esclavage? [*Shewing jewels.*]

FANNY.

Extremely handsome, indeed, and well fancied.

MISS STERLING.

What d'ye think of these bracelets? I shall have a miniature of
my father, set round with diamonds, to one, and Sir John's to
the other. – And this pair of earrings! set transparent! – Here,   30
the tops, you see, will take off to wear in a morning, or in an
undress. – How d'ye like them? [*Shews jewels.*]

FANNY.

Very much, I assure you. – Bless me; sister, you have a prodigious quantity of jewels – you'll be the very Queen of Diamonds.   30

MISS STERLING.

Ha! ha! ha! Very well, my dear! – I shall be as fine as a little
queen indeed. – I have a bouquet to come home tomorrow –
made up of diamonds, and rubies, and emeralds, and topazes,
and amethysts – jewels of all colours, green, red, blue, yellow,
intermixt – the prettiest thing you ever saw in your life! –   40
The jeweller says I shall set out with as many diamonds as any
body in town except Lady Brilliant, and Polly *What d'ye-call-
it*, Lord Squander's kept mistress.

FANNY.

But what are your wedding-cloaths, sister?

MISS STERLING.

Oh, white and silver, to be sure, you know. – I bought them   45
at Sir Joseph Lutestring's, and sat above an hour in the parlour
behind the shop consulting Lady Lutestring about gold and
silver stuffs, on purpose to mortify her.

FANNY.

Fie, sister! how could you be so abominably provoking?

---

26 esclavage] "A necklace composed of several rows of gold chain, beads, or
   jewels, so called from its resemblance to the fetters of a slave" (OED).
42-3 Polly *What d'ye-call-it*] A double allusion to Gay. The actress who created
   the part of Polly Peachum in *The Beggar's Opera*, Lavinia Fenton, was also the
   kept mistress of the Duke of Bolton. Gay also wrote *The What-d'ye-call it*, "a
   Tragi-Comi-Pastoral Farce," in 1715.

MISS STERLING.

Oh, I have no patience with the pride of your city-knights' 50
ladies. – Did you never observe the airs of Lady Lutestring
drest in the richest brocade out of her husband's shop, playing
crown-whist at Haberdasher's-Hall? – While the civil smirk-
ing Sir Joseph, with a snug wig trimmed round his broad face
as close as a new-cut yew-hedge, and his shoes so black that 55
they shine again, stands all day in his shop, fastened to his
counter like a bad shilling?

FANNY.

Indeed, indeed, sister, this is too much. – If you talk at this
rate, you will be absolutely a bye-word in the city. – You must
never venture on the inside of Temple-Bar again. 60

MISS STERLING.

Never do I desire it – never, my dear Fanny, I promise you. –
Oh, how I long to be transported to the dear regions of
Grosvenor-Square – far, far from the dull districts of Alders-
gate, Cheap, Candlewick, and Farringdon Without and
Within! – My heart goes pit-a-pat at the very idea of being 65

---

53 Crown-whist...Haberdasher's-Hall] Crown-whist is a variety of whist, a
forerunner of bridge. Haberdasher's-Hall was the central hall of the
haberdasher's guild in the City. Betsey's point is that Lady Lutestring's main
place of amusement is also a reminder that her husband, despite his title, is still
a tradesman.

59 bye-word] "an object of scorn or contempt" (OED).

60 Temple-Bar] One of the gates to the City. Temple-Bar originally stood at the
entrance of Fleet Street, near the present-day Law Courts, between Bell Yard
and Chancery Lane. Called "the bone in the throat of Fleet Street," it was
removed in this century to allow traffic to flow freely from Westminster into
the City proper.

63 Grosvenor-Square] In Mayfair, just south of Oxford Street. In the 1760s,
Grosvenor Square was at the heart of the fashionable new subdivision of
Mayfair, which grew as the nobility moved into the West End, away from the
filth and congestion of the City.

63-5 Aldersgate...Within] All sites within the City. *Aldersgate* stood near
Ironmongers' Hall and Smithfield meat market; ironically, it is now part of the
fashionable Barbican complex. *Cheap* is a contraction of Cheapside, the main
commercial street. *Candlewick* street, now Cannon Street, runs parallel to
Cheapside from St. Paul's Cathedral to Gracechurch Street. The parishes of
Farringdon Without and Within mark the western limit of Smithfield, and the
primarily mercantile district of Holborn. All these locations would be familiar
ground to a city dweller with an address in Gracechurch Street.

introduced at court – gilt chariot! – Pyeballed horses! – laced
liveries! – and then the whispers buzzing round the circle –
"Who is that young Lady! Who is she?" – "Lady Melvil,
Ma'am!" – Lady Melvil! my ears tingle at the sound. – And
then at dinner, instead of my father perpetually asking –   70
"Any news upon 'Change?" – to cry – well, Sir John! Anything new from Arthur's? – or – to say to some other woman
of quality, was it your Ladyship at the Dutchess of Rubber's
last night? – Did you call in at Lady Thunder's? In the im-
mensity of [the] croud I swear I did not see you – scarce a   75
soul at the opera last Saturday – shall I see you at Carlisle-
House next Thursday? – Oh, the dear Beau-Monde! I was
born to move in the sphere of the great world.

FANNY.

And so, in the midst of all this happiness, you have no compassion for me – no pity for us poor mortals in common life.   80

MISS STERLING [*Affectedly*].

You? – You're above pity. – You would not change conditions
with me – you're over head and ears in love, you know. – Nay,
for that matter, if Mr. Lovewell and you come together, as I
doubt not you will, you will live very comfortably, I dare say.
– He will mind his business, you'll employ yourself in the de-   85
lightful care of your family – and once in a season perhaps
you'll sit together in a front-box at a benefit play, as we used
to do at our dancing-master's, you know – and perhaps I may
meet you in the summer with some other citizens at Tunbridge. – For my part, I shall always entertain a proper regard   90

---

66 chariot] "A lighter kind of coach with only back seats" (Johnson).

72 Arthur's] A popular gaming-club, run by Robert Arthur, who was also the
proprietor of the more fashionable White's. Arthur's stood on Little St.
James's Street, part of the group of aristocratic clubs and gaming-rooms
clustered around St. James's Palace.

76-7 Carlisle-House] Seat of the Duke of Carlisle, and one of the more
fashionable places of amusement in the 1750s and 60s.

89-90 Tunbridge] One of the least fashionable of English spas. Although both
gentry and commoners patronised Tunbridge, those of fashion generally
preferred Bath. Betsey is suggesting here that Tunbridge is one of the few
places that she and her sister would both patronise.

for my relations. – You shan't want my countenance, I assure you.

FANNY.

Oh, you're too kind, sister!

Enter Mrs. Heidelberg.

MRS. HEIDELBERG [*At entring*].

Here this evening! I vow and pertest we shall scarce have enough time to provide for them. – [*To* Miss Sterling.] Oh, 95 my dear, I'm glad to see you're not quite in dish-abille. Lord Ogleby and Sir John Melvil will be here tonight.

MISS STERLING.

Tonight, Ma'am?

MRS. HEIDELBERG.

Yes, my dear, tonight. – Do put on a smarter cap, and change those ordinary ruffles! – Lord, I have such a deal to do, I shall 100 scarce have time to slip on my Italian lutestring. – Where is this dawdle of a housekeeper? –

Enter Mrs. Trusty.

Oh, here, Trusty! Do you know that people of qualaty are expected here this evening?

TRUSTY.

Yes, Ma'am. 105

MRS. HEIDELBERG.

Well. – Do you be sure now that everything is done in the most genteelest manner – and to the honour of the fammaly.

TRUSTY.

Yes, Ma'am.

MRS. HEIDELBERG.

Well – but mind what I say to you.

---

101 lutestring] "A kind of glossy silk fabric" (OED). The word is a derivation of "lustring," referring to the shimmering quality of the fabric. The fabric seems to have been used exclusively for women's clothing.

TRUSTY.

 Yes, Ma'am.   110

MRS. HEIDELBERG.

 His Lordship is to lie in the chintz bedchamber – d'ye hear? – And Sir John in the blue damask room. – His Lordship's valet-de-shamb in the opposite –

TRUSTY.

 But Mr. Lovewell is come down – and you know that's his room, Ma'am.   115

MRS. HEIDELBERG.

 Well – well – Mr. Lovewell may make shift – or get a bed at the George. – But hark ye, Trusty!

TRUSTY.

 Ma'am?

MRS. HEIDELBERG.

 Get the great dining room in order as soon as possible. Unpaper the curtains, take the civers off the couch and the chairs, 120 and put the china figures on the mantle-piece immediately.

TRUSTY.

 Yes, Ma'am.

MRS. HEIDELBERG.

 Be gone, then! Fly this instant! Where's my brother Sterling –

TRUSTY.

 Talking to the butler, Ma'am.

MRS. HEIDELBERG.

 Very well.   125

Exit Trusty.

 Miss Fanny! – I pertest I did not see you before. – Lord, child, what's the matter with you?

FANNY.

 With me? Nothing, Ma'am.

MRS. HEIDELBERG.

 Bless me! Why your face is as pale, and black, and yellow – of fifty colours, I pertest. – And then you have drest yourself as 130 loose and as big – I declare there is not such a thing to be seen now, as a young woman with a fine waist. – You all make yourself as round as Mrs. Deputy Barter. Go, child! – You

know the qualaty will be here by and by. – Go and make
yourself a little more fit to be seen.   135

Exit Fanny.

She is gone away in tears – absolutely crying, I vow and pert-
est. – This is ridicalous Love! We must put a stop to it. It
makes a perfect nataral of the girl.
MISS STERLING [*Affectedly*].
Poor soul! she can't help it.
MRS. HEIDELBERG.
Well, my dear! Now I shall have the opportunity of convinc-   140
ing you of the absurdity of what you was telling me concern-
ing Sir John Melvil's behaviour to you.
MISS STERLING.
Oh, it gives me no manner of uneasiness. But indeed, Ma'am,
I cannot be persuaded but that Sir John is an extremely cold
lover. Such distant civility, grave looks, and lukewarm profes-   145
sions of esteem for me and the whole family! I have heard of
flames and darts, but Sir John's is a passion of mere ice and
snow.
MRS. HEIDELBERG.
Oh, fie, my dear! I am pefectly ashamed of you. That's so like
the notions of your poor sister! What you complain of as   150
coldness and indiffarence, is nothing but extreme gentilaty of
his address, and exact pictur of the manners of qualaty.
MISS STERLING.
Oh, he is the very mirror of complaisance! Full of formal
bows and set speeches! – I declare, if there was any violent
passion on my side, I should be quite jealous of him.   155
MRS. HEIDELBERG.
I say jealus indeed. Jealus of who, pray?
MISS STERLING.
My sister Fanny. She seems a much greater favourite than I
am, and he pays her infinitely more attention, I assure you.
MRS. HEIDELBERG.
Lord! d'ye think a man of fashion, as he is, can't distinguish
between the genteel and the wulgar part of the famaly? – Be-   160
tween you and your sister, for instance – or me and my
brother? – Be advised by me, child! It is all politeness and

good-breeding. – Nobody knows the qualaty better than I
do.

MISS STERLING.

In my mind the old lord, his uncle, has ten times more gal-   165
lantry about him than Sir John. He is full of attentions to the
ladies, and smiles, and grins, and leers, and ogles, and fills
every wrinkle in his old wizen face with comical expressions
of tenderness. I think he would make an admirable sweet-
heart.   170

Enter Sterling.

STERLING [*At entring*].

No fish? – Why the pond was dragged but yesterday morning. – There's carp and tench in the boat. – Pox on't, if that
dog Lovewell had any thought, he would have brought down
a turbot, or some of the land-carriage mackarel.

MRS. HEIDELBERG.

Lord, brother, I am afraid his Lordship and Sir John will not   175
arrive while it's light.

STERLING.

I warrant you. – But pray, sister Heidelberg, let the turtle be
drest tomorrow, and some venison – and let the gardener cut
some pine-apples – and get out some ice. – I'll answer for
wine, I warrant you. – I'll give them such a glass of Cham-   180
pagne as they never drank in their lives – no, not at a Duke's
table.

MRS. HEIDELBERG.

Pray now, brother, mind how you behave. I am always in a
fright about you with people of qualaty. Take care that you
don't fall asleep directly after supper, as you commonly do.   185
Take a good deal of snuff; and that will keep you awake. –
And don't burst out with your horrible loud horse-laughs. It
is monstrous wulgar.

STERLING.

Never fear, sister! – Who have we here?

MRS. HEIDELBERG.

It is Mons. Cantoon, the Swish gentleman, that lives with his   190
Lordship, I vow and pertest.

Enter Canton.

STERLING.

Ah, Mounseer! your servant. – I am very glad to see you, Mounseer.

CANTON.

Mosh oblige to Mons. Sterling. – Ma'am, I am yours. – Matemoiselle, I am yours. [*Bowing round.*]   195

MRS. HEIDELBERG.

Your humble servant, Mr. Cantoon!

CANTON.

I kiss your hands, Matam!

STERLING.

Well, Mounseer! – and what news of your good family! – when are we to see his Lordship and Sir John?

CANTON.

Mons. Sterling! Milor Ogelby and Sir Jean Melvile will be   200
here in one quarter-hour.

STERLING.

I am glad to hear it.

MRS. HEIDELBERG.

O, I am perdigious glad to hear it. Being so late I was afeard of some accident. – Will you please to have any thing, Mr. Cantoon, after your journey?   205

CANTON.

No, I tank you, Ma'am.

MRS. HEIDELBERG.

Shall I go and shew you the apartments, Sir?

CANTON.

You do me great honeur, Ma'am.

MRS. HEIDELBERG.

Come then! – [*to* Miss Sterling.] – come, my dear!

Exeunt.

Manet Sterling.

STERLING.

Pox on't, it's almost dark. – It will be too late to go round the   210
garden this evening. – However, I will carry them to take a
peep at my fine canal at least, I am determined.

Exit.

ACT II

S C E N E , *an anti chamber to Lord Ogleby's bedchamber. – Table with*
chocolate, and small case for medicines.

Enter Brush, *my Lord's valet-de-chambre,*
and Sterling's *chamber-maid.*

BRUSH.

You shall stay, my dear, I insist upon it.

CHAMBERMAID.

Nay, pray, sir, don't be so positive; I can't stay indeed.

BRUSH.

You shall take one cup to better our acquaintance.

CHAMBERMAID.

I seldom drinks chocolate; and if I did, one has no satisfaction, with such apprehension about one – if my Lord should   5
wake, or the Swish gentleman should see one, or Madam
Heidelberg should know of it, I should be frighted to death –
besides, I have had my tea already this morning – [*In a fright.*]
I'm sure I hear my Lord.

BRUSH.

No, no, madam, don't flutter yourself – the moment my Lord   10
wakes, he rings his bell, which I answer sooner or later, as it
suits my convenience.

CHAMBERMAID.

But should he come upon us with ringing –

BRUSH.

I'll forgive him if he does. – This key [*takes a phial out of the*
case] locks him up till I please to let him out.   15

CHAMBERMAID.

Law, Sir! that's potecary's-stuff!

BRUSH.

It is so – but without this he can no more get out of bed –
than he can read without his spectacles. [*Sips.*] What with
qualms, age, rheumatism, and a few surfeits in his youth, he
must have a great deal of brushing, oyling, screwing, and   20
winding up to set him a going for the day.

CHAMBERMAID [*Sips*].

    That's prodigious indeed. – [*Sips.*] My Lord seems quite in a decay.

BRUSH.

    Yes, he's quite a spectacle, [*Sips.*] a mere corpse, till he is revived and refreshed from our little magazine here. – When   25
the restorative pills, and cordial waters warm his stomach, and get into his head, vanity frisks in his heart, and then he sets up for the lover, the rake, and the fine gentleman.

CHAMBERMAID [*Sips*].

    Poor gentleman! – [*Frightened.*] But should the Swish gentleman come upon us.   30

BRUSH.

    Why then the English gentleman would be very angry. – No foreigner must break in upon my privacy. [*Sips.*] But I can assure you Monsieur Canton is otherwise employed. – He is obliged to skim the cream of half a score newspapers for my Lord's breakfast – ha, ha, ha. Pray, madam, drink your cup   35
peaceably. – My Lord's chocolate is remarkably good, he won't touch a drop but what comes from Italy.

CHAMBERMAID [*Sipping*].

    'Tis very fine indeed! – [*Sips.*] and charmingly perfumed – it smells for all the world like our young ladies' dressing boxes.

BRUSH.

    You have an excellent taste, Madam, and I must beg of you to   40
accept a few cakes for your own drinking [*Takes 'em out of a drawer in the table.*], and in return I desire nothing but to taste the perfume of your lips. – [*Kisses her.*] – A small return of favours, Madam, will make, I hope, this country and retirement agreeable to both. [*He bows, she curtsies.*] Your young ladies are   45
fine girls, faith: [*Sips.*] tho' upon my soul, I am quite of my old lord's mind about them; and were I inclined to matrimony, I should take the youngest. [*Sips.*]

CHAMBERMAID.

    Miss Fanny's the most affablest and the most best natered creter!   50

BRUSH.

    And the eldest a little haughty or so –

CHAMBERMAID.

More haughtier and prouder than Saturn himself – but this I say quite confidential to you, for one would not hurt a young lady's marriage, you know. [*Sips.*]

BRUSH.

By no means, but you can't hurt it with us – we don't con- 55
sider tempers – we want money, Mrs. Nancy – give us enough of that, we'll abate you a great deal in other particulars – ha, ha, ha.

CHAMBERMAID.

Bless me, here's somebody [*Bell rings*] – O! 'tis my Lord. – Well, your servant, Mr. Brush. – I'll clean the cups in the next 60 room.

BRUSH.

Do so – but never mind the bell. – I shan't go this half hour. – Will you drink tea with me in the afternoon?

CHAMBERMAID.

Not for the world, Mr. Brush. – I'll be here to set all things to rights – but I must not drink tea indeed – and so your ser- 65 vant.

Exit Maid with tea board.

Bell rings again.

BRUSH.

It is impossible to stupify one's self in the country for a week without some little flirting with the Abigails: this is much the handsomest wench in the house, except the old citizen's youngest daughter, and I have not time enough to lay a plan 70 for Her. – [*Bell rings.*] And now I'll go to my Lord, for I have nothing else to do.

Going.

Enter Canton *with newspapers in his hand.*

---

68 Abigails] Generic term for female servants.

CANTON.

Monsieur Brush – Maistre Brush – My Lor stirra yet?

BRUSH.

He has just rung his bell – I am going to him.

Exit Brush.

CANTON.

Depechez vous donc. [*Puts on spectacles.*] I wish de Deviel had   75
all dese papiers – I forget as fast as I read. De Advertise put
out of my head de Gazette, de Gazette de Chronique, and so
dey all go l'un après l'autre. – I must get some nouvelle for
my Lor, or he'll be enragé contre moi. [*Reads in the papers.*]
Voyons! – Here is nothing but Anti-Sejanus & advertise –   80

Enter maid with chocolate things.

Vat you vant, child? –

CHAMBERMAID.

Only the chocolate things, sir.

CANTON.

O, ver well – dat is a good girl – and ver prit too!

Exit Maid.

LORD OGLEBY [*Within*].

Canton, he, he – [*Coughs.*] – Canton!

CANTON.

I come, my Lor – vat shall I do? – I have no news. – He vil   85
make great tintamarre! –

LORD OGLEBY [*Within*].

Canton, I say, Canton! Where are you? –

Enter Lord Ogleby *leaning on* Brush.

___

86 tintamarre] "A great uprorar, full of confusion and disorder." (Académie
Française)

CANTON.

Here, My Lor, I ask pardon, my Lor, I have not finish de papiers –

LORD OGLEBY.

Dem your pardon, and your papers – I want you here, Canton. 90

CANTON.

Den I run, dat is all. [*Shuffles along.* – Lord Ogleby *leans upon* Canton *too, and comes forward.*]

LORD OGLEBY.

You Swiss are the most unaccountable mixture – you have the language and impertinence of the French, with the lazi- 95
ness of Dutchmen.

CANTON.

'Tis very true, my Lor – I can't help –

LORD OGLEBY [*Cries out*].

O Diavolo!

CANTON.

You are not in pain, I hope, my Lor.

LORD OGLEBY.

Indeed but I am, my Lor. – That vulgar fellow Sterling, with 100
his city politeness, would force me down his slope last night
to see a clay-coloured ditch, which he calls a canal; and what
with the dew, and the east-wind, my hips and shoulders are
absolutely screwed to my body.

CANTON.

A littel veritable eau d'arquibusade vil set all to right again. 105
[*My Lord sits down,* Brush *gives chocolate.*]

LORD OGLEBY.

Where are the palsy drops, Brush?

BRUSH.

Here, my Lord [*Pouring out.*]

LORD OGLEBY.

Quelle nouvelle avez vous, Canton?

CANTON.

A great deal of papier, but no news at all.

---

98 O Diavolo] "O the Devil" (Italian).

LORD OGLEBY.

What nothing at all, you stupid fellow? 110

CANTON.

Yes, my Lor, I have littel advertise here vil give you more plaisir den all de lyes about noting at all. La voilà! [*Puts on his spectacles.*]

LORD OGLEBY.

Come, read it, Canton, with good emphasis, and good discretion.

CANTON.

I vil, my Lor. – [Canton *reads.*] Dere is no question, but dat de 115 Cosmetique Royale vil utterlie take away all heats, pimps, frecks & oder eruptions of de skin, and likewise de wrinque of old age, &c. &c. – A great deal mor, my Lor – be sure to ask for de Cosmetique Royale, signed by de Docteur own hand. – Dere is more raison for dis caution dan good men vil tink. 120 – Eh bien, my Lor!

LORD OGLEBY.

Eh bien, Canton! – Will you purchase any?

CANTON.

For you, my Lor?

LORD OGLEBY.

For me, you old puppy! for what?

CANTON.

My Lor? 125

LORD OGLEBY.

Do I want cosmeticks?

CANTON.

My Lor!

LORD OGLEBY.

Look in my face – come, be sincere. – Does it want the assistance of art?

CANTON [*With his spectacles*].

En verité, non. – 'Tis very smoose and brillian – but I tote 130 dat you might take a little by way of prevention.

LORD OGLEBY.

You thought like an old fool, Monsieur, as you generally do. – The surfeit-water, Brush! [Brush *pours out.*] What do you think, Brush, of this family we are going to be connected with? – Eh? 135

BRUSH [*Giving the surfeit-water*].

Very well to marry in, my Lord; but it would not do to live with.

LORD OGLEBY.

You are right, Brush. – There is no washing the Blackamoor white. – Mr. Sterling will never get rid of Black-Fryars, always taste of the Borachio – and the poor woman his sister is 140 so busy and so notable, to make one welcome, that I have not yet got over her first reception; it almost amounted to suffocation! I think the daughters are tolerable. – Where's my cephalick snuff? [Brush *gives him a box.*]

CANTON.

Dey tink so of you, my Lor, for dey look at noting else, ma 145 foi.

LORD OGLEBY.

Did they? – Why, I think they did a little. – Where's my glass? [Brush *puts one on the table.*] The youngest is delectable. [*Takes snuff.*]

CANTON.

O, ouy, my Lor – very delect, inteed; she make doux yeux at you, my Lor. 150

LORD OGLEBY.

She was particular – the eldest, my nephew's lady, will be a most valuable wife; she has all the vulgar spirits of her father, and aunt, happily blended with the termagant qualities of her deceased mother. – Some pepper-mint water, Brush! – How

---

SD surfeit-water] "Cold distilled poppywater," according to one definition in Johnson. Surfeit-water is any liquid – no doubt an emetic – that cures the effects of overeating.

139 Black-Fryars] Area of London just south of Fleet Street. Earlier in the century, the open sewer of Fleet Ditch ran through Blackfriars, and near the mouth of the ditch stood the notorious Bridewell prison.

140 Borachio] An obscure term. Pedicord and Bergmann speculate that Ogleby means "a wine merchant," after the Spanish "borachio," for "wine-bag." If so, then Garrick is indulging in a bit of self-parody, since he began his professional life as a wine-merchant.

149 doux yeux] The Académie Française defines *faire les doux yeux* as, *Composer les regards de telle forte que les yeux en paroisent plus doux.*

happy it is, Cant, for young ladies in general that people of   155
quality overlook everything in a marriage contract but their
fortune.

CANTON.

C'est bien heureux, et commode aussi.

LORD OGLEBY.

Brush, give me that pamphlet by my bedside. [*Brush goes for
it.*] Canton, do you wait in the anti-chamber, and let nobody   160
interrupt me till I call you.

CANTON.

Mush goot may do your Lordship!

LORD OGLEBY [*To* Brush, *who brings the pamphlet*].

And now, Brush, leave me a little to my studies.

Exit Brush.

LORD OGLEBY [*Alone*].

What can I possibly do among these women here, with this
confounded rheumatism? It is a most grievous enemy to gal-   165
lantry and address. – [*Gets off his chair.*] He! – Courage, my
Lor! By heavens, I'm another creature. – [*Hums and dances a
little.*] It will do, faith. – Bravo, my Lor! These girls have absolutely inspired me. – If they are for a game of romps. – Me
voila pret! [*Sings and dances.*] O – that's an ugly twinge – but   170
it's gone. – I have rather too much of the lily this morning in
my complexion; a faint tincture of the rose will give a delicate spirit to my eyes for the day. [*Unlocks a drawer at the bottom of the glass and takes out rouge; while he's painting himself, a
knocking at the door.*] Who's there! I won't be disturbed.   175

CANTON [*Without*].

My Lor, my Lor, here is Monsieur Sterling to pay his devoir
to you this morn in your chambre.

LORD OGLEBY [*Softly*].

What a fellow! – [*Aloud.*] I am extreamly honoured by Mr.
Sterling. – Why don't you see him in, Monsieur? – [*Aside.*] I
wish he was at the bottom of his stinking canal. – [*Door*   180
opens.] Oh, my dear Mr. Sterling, you do me a great deal of
honour.

Enter Sterling *and* Lovewell.

STERLING.

I hope, my Lord, that your Lordship slept well in the night – I
believe there are no better beds in Europe than I have – I
spare no pains to get 'em, nor money to buy 'em. – His Maj-   185
esty, God bless him, don't sleep upon a better out of his palace; and if I had said *in* too, I hope no treason, my Lord.

LORD OGLEBY.

Your beds are like everything else about you, incomparable! –
They not only make one rest well, but give one spirits, Mr.
Sterling.   190

STERLING.

What say you then, my Lord, to another walk in the garden?
You must see my water by daylight, and my walks, and my
slopes, and my clumps, and my bridge, and my flowering
trees, and my bed of Dutch tulips. – Matters looked but dim
last night, my Lord; I feel the dew in my great toe – but I   195
would put on a cut shoe that I might be able to walk you
about. – I may be laid up tomorrow.

LORD OGLEBY [*Aside*].

I pray heaven you may!

STERLING.

What say you, my Lord?

LORD OGLEBY.

I was saying, Sir, that I was in hopes of seeing the young ladies   200
at breakfast: Mr. Sterling, they are, in my mind, the finest tulips in this part of the world – he, he.

CANTON.

Bravissimo, my Lor! – ha, ha, he.

STERLING.

They shall meet your Lordship in the garden – we won't lose
our walk for them; I'll take you a little round before breakfast,   205
and a larger before dinner, and in the evening you shall go the
Grand Tower, as I call it, ha, ha, ha.

LORD OGLEBY.

Not a foot, I hope, Mr. Sterling – consider your gout, my
good friend. – You'll certainly be laid by the heels for your
politeness – he, he, he.   210

CANTON.

Ha, ha, ha – 'tis admirable, en verité! [*Laughing very heartily.*]

STERLING.

    If my young man [*To* Lovewell.] here would but laugh at my jokes, which he ought to do, as Mounseer does at yours, my Lord, we should be all life and mirth.

LORD OGLEBY.

    What say you, Cant, will you take my kinsman under your 215 tuition? you have certainly the most companionable laugh I ever met with, and never out of tune.

CANTON.

    But when your Lorship is out of spirits.

LORD OGLEBY.

    Well said, Cant! – But here comes my nephew, to play his part. 220

Enter Sir John Melvil.

    Well, Sir John, what news from the island of Love? have you been sighing and serenading this morning?

SIR JOHN.

    I am glad to see your Lordship in such spirits this morning.

LORD OGLEBY.

    I'm sorry to see you so dull, Sir. – What poor things, Mr. Sterling, these *very* young fellows are! They make love with faces, 225 as if they were burying the dead – though, indeed, a marriage sometimes may be properly called a burying of the living – eh, Mr. Sterling? –

STERLING.

    Not if they have enough to live upon, my Lord – ha, ha, ha.

CANTON.

    Dat is all Monsieur Sterling tink of. 230

SIR JOHN [*Apart to* Lovewell].

    Prithee, Lovewell, come with me into the garden; I have something of consequence for you, and I must communicate it directly.

LOVEWELL [*Apart to* Sir John].

    We'll go together. – [*Aloud.*] If your Lordship and Mr. Sterling please, we'll prepare the ladies to attend you in the garden. 235

Exeunt Sir John *and* Lovewell.

STERLING.

My girls are always ready, I make 'em rise soon and to-bed early; their husbands shall have 'em with good constitutions, and good fortunes, if they have nothing else, my Lord.

LORD OGLEBY.

Fine things, Mr. Sterling!

STERLING.

Fine things, indeed, my Lord! – Ah, my Lord, had not you   240
run off your speed in your youth, you had not been so crippled in your age, my Lord.

LORD OGLEBY.

Very pleasant, I protest – [*Half laughing.*] – he, he, he.

STERLING.

Here's Mounseer now, I suppose, is pretty near your Lordship's standing; but having little to eat, and little to spend, in   245
his own country, he'll wear three of your Lordship out – eating and drinking kills us all.

LORD OGLEBY.

Very pleasant, I protest. – [*Aside.*] What a vulgar dog!

CANTON.

My Lor so old as me! – He is shicken to me – and look like a boy to pauvre me.   250

STERLING.

Ha, ha, ha. Well said, Mounseer – keep to that and you'll live in any country of the world. – Ha, ha, ha. But, my Lord, I will wait upon you into the garden: we have but a little time to breakfast. – I'll go for my hat and cane, fetch a little walk with you, my Lord, and then for the hot rolls and butter!   255

Exit Sterling.

LORD OGLEBY.

I shall attend you with pleasure. – Hot rolls and butter, in July! – I sweat with the thoughts of it. – What a strange beast it is!

CANTON.

C'est un barbare.

LORD OGLEBY.

> He is a vulgar dog, and if there was not so much money in 260
> the family, which I can't do without, I would leave him and
> his hot rolls and butter directly. – Come along, Monsieur!

Exeunt

SCENE changes to the Garden. [II.ii]
Enter Sir John Melvil, *and* Lovewell.

LOVEWELL.

> In my room this morning? Impossible.

SIR JOHN.

> Before five this morning, I promise you.

LOVEWELL.

> On what occasion?

SIR JOHN.

> I was so anxious to disclose my mind to you that I could not
> sleep in my bed. – But I found that you could not sleep nei- 5
> ther. – The bird was flown, and the nest long since cold. –
> Where was you, Lovewell?

LOVEWELL.

> Pooh! prithee! ridiculous!

SIR JOHN.

> Come now! which was it? Miss Sterling's maid? a pretty little
> rogue! – or Miss Fanny's Abigail? A sweet soul too! – or – 10

LOVEWELL.

> Nay, nay, leave trifling, and tell me your business.

SIR JOHN.

> Well, but where was you, Lovewell?

LOVEWELL.

> Walking – writing – what signifies where I was?

SIR JOHN.

> Walking! Yes, I dare say. It rained as hard as it could pour.
> Sweet refreshing showers to walk in! No, no Lovewell. – 15
> Now would I give twenty pound to know which of the
> maids –

LOVEWELL.

> But your business! your business, Sir John!

SIR JOHN.

Let me a little into the secrets of the family.

LOVEWELL.

Psha!   20

SIR JOHN.

Poor Lovewell! he can't bear it, I see. She charged you not to
kiss and tell. – Eh, Lovewell! However, though you will not
honour me with your confidence, I'll venture to trust you
with mine. – What d'ye think of Miss Sterling?

LOVEWELL.

What do I think of Miss Sterling?   25

SIR JOHN.

Ay; what d'ye think of her?

LOVEWELL.

An odd question! – But I think her a smart, lively girl, full of
mirth and sprightliness.

SIR JOHN.

All mischief and malice, I doubt.

LOVEWELL.

How?   30

SIR JOHN.

But her person – what d'ye think of that?

LOVEWELL.

Pretty and agreeable.

SIR JOHN.

A little grisette thing.

LOVEWELL.

What is the meaning of all this?

SIR JOHN.

I'll tell you. You must know, Lovewell, that notwithstanding   35
all appearances – [Seeing Lord Ogleby, &c.] We are interrupted. – When they are gone, I'll explain.

---

33 grisette] Term for a young girl, or, as the Académie suggests, *une jeune femme
de basse condition.* The term has a slightly bawdy ring to it, which may
determine how Lovewell's question is spoken.

Enter Lord Ogleby, Sterling, Mrs. Heidelberg,
Miss Sterling, *and* Fanny.

LORD OGLEBY.

Great improvements indeed, Mr. Sterling! Wonderful improvements! The four seasons in lead, the flying Mercury, and
the basin with Neptune in the middle, are all in the very ex-   40
treme of fine taste. You have as many rich figures as the man
at Hyde-Park Corner.

STERLING.

The chief pleasure of a country house is to make improvements, you know, my Lord. I spare no expence, not I. – This is
quite another-guess sort of a place than it was when I first   45
took it, my Lord. We were surrounded with trees. I cut down
above fifty to make the lawn before the house, and let in the
wind and the sun – smack-smooth – as you see. – Then I
made a green-house out of the old laundry, and turned the
brew-house into a pinery. – The high octagon summer-   50
house, you see yonder, is raised on the mast of a ship, given
me by an East-India captain who has turned many a thousand of my money. It commands the whole road. All the
coaches and chariots, and chaises, pass and repass under your
eye. I'll mount you up there in the afternoon, my Lord. 'Tis   55
the pleasantest place in the world to take a pipe and a bottle,
– and so you shall say, my Lord.

LORD OGLEBY.

Ay – or a bowl of punch or a can of flip, Mr. Sterling! – for it
looks like a cabin in the air. – If flying chairs were in use, the
captain might make a voyage to the Indies in it still, if he had   60
but a fair wind.

CANTON.

Ha! ha! ha! ha!

MRS. HEIDELBERG.

My brother's a little comacal in his ideas, my Lord! – But
you'll excuse him. – I have a little gothic dairy, fitted up en-

---

58 flip] Also spelled "flipp." "A liquor much used in ships, made by mixing beer
with spirits and sugar" (Johnson).

tirely in my own taste. – In the evening I shall hope for the   65
honour of your Lordship's company to take a dish of tea
there, or a sullabub warm from the cow.

LORD OGLEBY.

I have every moment a fresh opportunity of admiring the
elegance of Mrs. Heidelberg – the very flower of delicacy,
and cream of politeness.   70

MRS. HEIDELBERG.

Oh, my Lord!

LORD OGLEBY.   [*Leering at each other.*]

Oh, Madam!

STERLING.

How d'ye like these close walks, my Lord?

LORD OGLEBY.

A most excellent serpentine! It forms a perfect maze, and
winds like a true-lover's knot.   75

STERLING.

Ay, here's none of your strait lines here – but all taste – zig-
zag – crinkum-crankum – in and out – right and left – to and
again – twisting and turning like a worm, my Lord!

LORD OGLEBY.

Admirably laid out indeed, Mr. Sterling! One can hardly see
an inch beyond one's nose any where in these walks. – You   80
are a most excellent œconomist of your land, and make a little go a great way. – It lies together in as small parcels as if it
was placed in pots out at your window in Gracechurch-
street.

CANTON.

Ha! ha! ha! ha!   85

LORD OGLEBY.

What d'ye laugh at, Canton?

---

67 sullabub] Syllabub, a rustic drink made with wine, cream, and sugar. Syllabubs
    can have the consistency either of milkshakes or of stiff custards.
83-4 Gracechurch-street] City street that runs north from the Monument on
    Fish St. Hill to Cornhill Street, a few yards away from the Royal Exchange.
    Sterling's City address.

CANTON.

Ah! que cette similitude est drôle! So clever what you say, mi Lor!

LORD OGLEBY [*To* Fanny].

You seem mightily engaged, Madam. What are those pretty hands so busily employed about? 90

FANNY.

Only making up a nosegay, my Lord! – Will your Lordship do me the honour of accepting it? [*Presenting it.*]

LORD OGLEBY.

I'll wear it next my heart, Madam! – [*Apart.*] I see the young creature doats on me.

MISS STERLING.

Lord, sister! – you've loaded his Lordship with a bunch of 95 flowers as big as the cook or the nurse carry to town on Monday morning for a beaupot. – Will your Lordship give leave to present you with this rose and a sprig of sweet-briar?

LORD OGLEBY.

The truest emblems of yourself, Madam! All sweetness and poignancy. – [*Apart.*] A little jealous, poor soul! 100

STERLING.

Now, my Lord, if you please, I'll carry you to see my Ruins.

MRS. HEIDELBERG.

You'll absolutely fatigue his Lordship with overwalking, Brother!

LORD OGLEBY.

Not at all, Madam! We're in the garden of Eden, you know; in the region of perpetual spring, youth, and beauty. [*Leering at* 105 *the women.*]

MRS. HEIDELBERG [*Apart*].

Quite the man of qualaty, I pertest.

CANTON.

Take my arm, mi Lor! [Lord Ogleby *leans on him.*]

STERLING.

I'll only shew his Lordship my ruins, and the cascade, and the Chinese bridge, and then we'll go to breakfast.

LORD OGLEBY.

Ruins, did you say, Mr. Sterling? 110

STERLING.

Ay, ruins, my Lord! And they are reckoned very fine ones too. You would think them ready to tumble on your head. It has just cost me a hundred and fifty pounds to put my ruins in thorough repair. – This way, if your Lordship pleases.

LORD OGLEBY [*Going, stops*].

What steeple's that we see yonder? The parish-church, I suppose. 115

STERLING.

Ha! ha! ha! that's admirable. It is no church at all, my Lord! It is a spire that I have built against a tree, a field or two off, to terminate the prospect. One must always have a church, or an obelisk, or a something, to terminate the prospect, you know. 120 That's a rule in taste, my Lord.

LORD OGLEBY.

Very ingenious, indeed! For my part, I desire no finer prospect, than this I see before me. [*Leering at the women.*] – Simple, yet varied; bounded, yet extensive. – Get away, Canton! [*Pushing away* Canton.] I want no assistance. – I'll walk with 125 the ladies.

CANTON.

This way, my Lord.

LORD OGLEBY.

Lead on, Sir! – We young folks here will follow you. – Madam! – Miss Sterling! – Miss Fanny! I attend you.

Exit after Sterling, *gallanting the ladies.*

CANTON [*Following*].

He is cock o' de game, ma foy! 130

Exit.
Manent Sir John Melvil, *and* Lovewell.

---

130 cock o' de game] Canton's version of "cock of the walk." I have not traced the variant of this expression in any slang dictionary, and assume it to be Canton's own invention.

SIR JOHN.

At length, thank heaven, I have an opportunity to unbosom.
– I know you are faithful, Lovewell, and flatter myself you
would rejoice to serve me.

LOVEWELL.

Be assured, you may depend on me.

SIR JOHN.

You must know, then, notwithstanding all appearances, that   135
this treaty of marriage between Miss Sterling and me will
come to nothing.

LOVEWELL.

How!

SIR JOHN.

It will be no match, Lovewell.

LOVEWELL.

No match?   140

SIR JOHN.

No.

LOVEWELL.

You amaze me. What should prevent it?

SIR JOHN.

I.

LOVEWELL.

You! Wherefore?

SIR JOHN.

I don't like her.   145

LOVEWELL.

Very plain indeed! I never supposed that you was extremely
devoted to her from inclination, but thought you always considered it as a matter of convenience, rather than affection.

SIR JOHN.

Very true. I came into the family without any impressions on
my mind – with an unimpassioned indifference ready to re-   150
ceive one woman as soon as another. I looked upon love, serious, sober love, as a chimæra and marriage as a thing of
course, as you know most people do. But I, who was lately so
great an infidel in love, am now one of its sincerest votaries. –
In short, my defection from Miss Sterling proceeds from the   155
violence of my attachment to another.

LOVEWELL.

Another! So! so! Here will be fine work. And pray, who is she?

SIR JOHN.

Who is she? Who can she be? but Fanny, the tender, amiable, engaging Fanny.   160

LOVEWELL.

Fanny! What Fanny?

SIR JOHN.

Fanny Sterling. Her sister. – Is not she an angel, Lovewell?

LOVEWELL.

Her sister? Confusion! – You must not think of it, Sir John.

SIR JOHN.

Not think of it? I can think of nothing else. Nay, tell me, Lovewell! was it possible for me to be in a perpetual inter-   165 course with two such objects as Fanny and her sister, and not find my heart led by insensible attraction towards Her? – You seem confounded. – Why don't you answer me?

LOVEWELL.

Indeed, Sir John, this event gives me infinite concern.

SIR JOHN.

Why so? – Is not she an angel, Lovewell?   170

LOVEWELL.

I foresee that it must produce the worst consequences. Consider the confusion that it must unavoidably create. Let me persuade you to drop these thoughts in time.

SIR JOHN.

Never – never, Lovewell!

LOVEWELL.

You have gone too far to recede. A negotiation, so nearly   175 concluded, cannot be broken off with any grace. The lawyers, you know, are hourly expected; the preliminaries almost finally settled between Lord Ogleby and Mr. Sterling; and Miss Sterling herself ready to receive you as a husband.

SIR JOHN.

Why the banns have been published, and nobody has forbid-   180 den them, 'tis true – but you know either of the parties may change their minds even after they enter the church.

LOVEWELL.

You think too lightly of this matter. To carry your addresses
so far — and then to desert her — and for her sister too! — It
will be such an affront to the family, that they can never put   185
up with it.

SIR JOHN.

I don't think so: for as to my transferring my passion from her
to her sister, so much the better! — For then, you know, I
don't carry my affections out of the family.

LOVEWELL.

Nay, but prithee be serious, and think the better of it.   190

SIR JOHN.

I have thought the better of it already, you see. Tell me hon-
estly, Lovewell! can you blame me? Is there any comparison
between them?

LOVEWELL.

As to that now — why that — that is just — just as it may strike
different people. There are many admirers of Miss Sterling's   195
vivacity.

SIR JOHN.

Vivacity! A medley of Cheapside pertness, and Whitechapel
pride. — No — no — if I do go so far into the city for the wed-
ding-dinner, it shall be upon turtle, at least.

LOVEWELL.

But, I see no probability of success; for granting that Mr. Ster-   200
ling would have consented to it at first, he cannot listen to it
now. Why did not you break this affair to the family before?

SIR JOHN.

Under such embarrassed circumstances as I have been, can
you wonder at my irresolution or perplexity? Nothing but
despair, the fear of losing my dear Fanny, could bring me to a   205
declaration even now: and yet I think I know Mr. Sterling so
well, that, strange as my proposal may appear, if I can make it

---

197 Whitechapel] For Cheapside, see above. Whitechapel marks the eastern
boundary of the City; even in the eighteenth-century it was a notoriously
crime-ridden district.

advantageous to him as a money-transaction, as I am sure I
can, he will certainly come into it.

LOVEWELL.

But even suppose he should, which I very much doubt, I   210
don't think Fanny herself would listen to your addresses.

SIR JOHN.

You are deceived a little in that particular.

LOVEWELL.

You'll find I am in the right.

SIR JOHN.

I have some little reason to think otherwise.

LOVEWELL.

You have not declared your passion to her already?   215

SIR JOHN.

Yes, I have.

LOVEWELL.

Indeed! – And – and – how did she receive it?

SIR JOHN.

I think it is not very easy to make my addresses to any
woman, without receiving some little encouragement.

LOVEWELL.

Encouragement! Did she give you any encouragement?   220

SIR JOHN.

I don't know what you call encouragement – but she blushed
– and cried – and desired me not to think of it any more: –
upon which I prest her hand – kissed it – swore she was an
angel – and I could see it tickled her to the soul.

LOVEWELL.

And did she express no surprise at your declaration?   225

SIR JOHN.

Why, faith, to say the truth, she was a little surprised – and she
got away from me, too, before I could thoroughly explain
myself. If I should not meet with an opportunity of speaking
to her, I must get you to deliver a letter from me.

LOVEWELL.

I! – A letter! – I had rather have nothing –   230

SIR JOHN.

Nay, you promised me your assistance – and I am sure you
cannot scruple to make yourself useful on such an occasion. –
You may, without suspicion, acquaint her verbally of my de-

termined affection for her, and that I am resolved to ask her
father's consent.   235

LOVEWELL.

As to that, I – your commands, you know – that is, if she. –
Indeed, Sir John, I think you are in the wrong.

SIR JOHN.

Well – well – that's my concern. – Ha! There she goes, by
heaven! – along that walk yonder, d'ye see? I'll go to her immediately.   240

LOVEWELL.

You are too precipitate. Consider what you are doing.

SIR JOHN.

I would not lose this opportunity for the universe.

LOVEWELL.

Nay, pray don't go! Your violence and eagerness may overcome her spirits. – The shock will be too much for her. [De-
taining him.]

SIR JOHN.

Nothing shall prevent me. – Ha! Now she turns into another   245
walk. – Let me go! [Breaks from him.] I shall lose her. – [Going,
turns back.] Be sure now to keep out of the way! If you interrupt us, I shall never forgive you.

Exit hastily.

LOVEWELL [*Alone*].

'Sdeath! I can't bear this. In love with my wife! Acquaint me
with his passion for her! Make his addresses before my face! –   250
I shall break out before my time. – This was the meaning of
Fanny's uneasiness. She could not encourage him – I am sure
she could not. – Ha! They are turning into the walk and
coming this way. – Shall I leave the place? – Leave him to sol-
licit my wife! I can't submit to it. – They come nearer and   255
nearer. – If I stay it will look suspicious. – It may betray us,
and incense him. – They are here – I must go. I am the most
unfortunate fellow in the world.

Exit.
Enter Fanny *and* Sir John.

FANNY.

Leave me, Sir John, I beseech you leave me! – nay, why will
you persist to follow me with idle sollicitations, which are an   260
affront to my character and an injury to your own honour?
SIR JOHN.

I know your delicacy, and tremble to offend it: but let the urgency of the occasion be my excuse! Consider, Madam, that
the future happiness of my life depends on my present appli-
cation to you! Consider that this day you must determine my   265
fate; and these are perhaps the only moments left me to in-
cline you to warrant my passion and to intreat you not to oppose the proposals I mean to open to your father.
FANNY.

For shame, for shame, Sir John! Think of your previous engagements! Think of your own situation, and think of mine!   270
– What have you discovered in my conduct that might encourage you to so bold a declaration? I am shocked that you
should venture to say so much, and blush that I should even
dare to give it a hearing. – Let me be gone!
SIR JOHN.

Nay, stay, Madam! but one moment! – Your sensibility is too   275
great. – Engagements! what engagements have even been
pretended on either side than those of family-convenience? I
went on in the trammels of matrimonial negotiation with a
blind submission to your father and Lord Ogleby; but my
heart soon claimed a right to be consulted. It has devoted it-   280
self to you, and obliges me to plead earnestly for the same
tender interest in your's.
FANNY.

Have a care, Sir John! Do not mistake a depraved will for a
virtuous inclination. By these common pretences of the
heart, half of our sex are made fools, and a greater part of   285
yours despise them for it.
SIR JOHN.

Affection, you will allow, is involuntary. We cannot always direct it to the object on which it should fix. – But when it is

---

275 sensibility] "Quickness of sensation...and perception" (Johnson).

once inviolably attached, inviolably as mine is to you, it often creates reciprocal affection. – When I last urged you on this   290
subject, you heard me with more temper, and I hoped with some compassion.

FANNY.

You deceived yourself. If I forebore to exert a proper spirit, nay, if I did not even express the quickest resentment of your behaviour, it was only in consideration of the respect I wish   295
to pay you, in honour to my sister: and be assured, Sir, woman as I am, that my vanity could reap no pleasure from a triumph that must result from the blackest treachery to her. [*Going.*]

SIR JOHN.

One word, and I have done. – [*Stopping her.*] Your impatience and anxiety, and the urgency of the occasion, oblige me to be   300
brief and explicit with you. – I appeal therefore from your delicacy to your justice. – Your sister, I verily believe, neither entertains any real affection for me, or tenderness for you. – Your father, I am inclined to think, is not much concerned by means of which of his daughters the families are united. –   305
Now, as they cannot, shall not be connected otherwise than by my union with you, why will you, from a false delicacy, oppose a measure so conducive to my happiness and, I hope, your own? – I love you, most passionately and sincerely love you – and hope to propose terms agreeable to Mr. Sterling. –   310
If then you don't absolutely loath, abhor, and scorn me – if there is no other happier man –

FANNY.

Hear me, Sir! Hear my final determination. – Were my father and sister as insensible as you are pleased to represent them; were my heart forever to remain disengaged to any other – I   315
could not listen to your proposals. – What! You on the very eve of a marriage with my sister; I living under the same roof with her, bound not only by laws of friendship and hospitality, but even the ties of blood, to contribute to her happiness, – and not to conspire against her peace – the peace of a   320
whole family – and that my own too! Away! – away, Sir John! – At such a time, and in such circumstances, your addresses only inspire me with horror. – Nay, you must detain me no longer. – I will go.

SIR JOHN.

    Do not leave me in absolute despair! – Give me a glimpse of   325
hope! [*Falling on his knees.*]

FANNY.

    I cannot. Pray, Sir John! [*Struggling to go.*]

SIR JOHN.

    Shall this hand be given to another? [*Kissing her hand.*] No – I
cannot endure it. – My whole soul is yours, and the whole
happiness of my life is in your power.   330

Enter Miss Sterling.

FANNY.

    Ha! my sister is here. Rise for shame, Sir John!

SIR JOHN [*Rising*].

    Miss Sterling!

MISS STERLING.

    I beg pardon, Sir! – You'll excuse me, Madam! – I have broke
in upon you a little unopportunely, I believe. – But I did not
mean to interrupt you – I only came, Sir, to let you know   335
that breakfast waits, if you have finished your morning's de-
votions.

SIR JOHN.

    I am very sensible, Miss Sterling, that this may appear particu-
lar, but –

MISS STERLING.

    Oh dear, Sir John, don't put yourself to the trouble of an   340
apology. The thing explains itself.

SIR JOHN.

    It will soon, Madam! – In the mean time I can only assure
you of my profound respect and esteem for you, and make no
doubt of convincing Mr. Sterling of the honour and integrity
of my intentions. And – and – your humble servant, Madam!   345

Exit, in confusion.
Manent Fanny, *and* Miss Sterling.

MISS STERLING.

    Respect? – Insolence! – Esteem? – Very fine truly! – And you,
Madam! my sweet, delicate, innocent, sentimental sister! will

you convince my papa too of the integrity of your intentions?

FANNY.

Do not upbraid me, my dear sister! Indeed, I don't deserve it. 350
Believe me, you can't be more offended at his behaviour than
I am, and I am sure it cannot make you half so miserable.

MISS STERLING.

Make me miserable! You are mightily deceived, Madam! It
gives me no sort of uneasiness, I assure you. – A base fellow! –
As for you, Miss! the pretended softness of your disposition, 355
your artful good-nature, never imposed upon me. I always
knew you to be sly, and envious, and deceitful.

FANNY.

Indeed you wrong me.

MISS STERLING.

Oh, you are all goodness, to be sure! – Did not I find him on
his knees before you? Did not I see him kiss your sweet hand? 360
Did I not hear his protestations? Was not I witness of your
dissembled modesty? – No – no, my dear! don't imagine that
you can make a fool of your elder sister so easily.

FANNY.

Sir John, I own, is to blame; but I am above the thought of
doing you the least injury. 365

MISS STERLING.

We shall try that, Madam! – I hope, Miss, you'll be able to
give a better account to my papa and my aunt – for they shall
both know of this matter, I promise you.

Exit.

FANNY [*Alone*].

How unhappy I am! My distresses multiply upon me. – Mr.
Lovewell must now become acquainted with Sir John's be- 370
haviour to me – and in a manner that may add to his uneasiness. – My father, instead of being disposed by fortunate circumstances to forgive any transgression, will be previously
incensed against me. – My sister and my aunt will become ir-
reconcilably my enemies, and rejoice in my disgrace. – Yet, at 375
all events, I am determined on a discovery. I dread it, and am

resolved to hasten it. It is surrounded with more horrors every instant, as it appears every instant more necessary.

Exit.

ACT III

A hall.

Enter a servant leading in Serjeant Flower *and* Counsellors Travers *and* Truman – *all booted.*

SERVANT.

This way, if you please, gentlemen! my master is at breakfast with the family at present – but I'll let him know, and he will wait on you immediately.

FLOWER.

Mighty well, young man, mighty well.

SERVANT.

Please to favour me with your names, gentlemen.   5

FLOWER.

Let Mr. Sterling know, that Mr. Serjeant Flower and two other gentlemen of the bar, are come to wait on him according to his appointment.

SERVANT.

I will, sir. [*Going.*]

FLOWER.

And harkee, young man! [Servant *returns.*] Desire my servant   10
– Mr. Serjeant Flower's servant – to bring in my green and gold saddle-cloth and pistols, and lay them down here in the hall with my portmanteau.

SERVANT.

I will, sir.

Exit.

FLOWER.

Well, gentlemen! the settling these marriage-articles falls   15
conveniently enough, almost just on the eve of the circuits. –

---

16 circuits] Divisions of England and Wales to which justices would travel twice a year to hear cases. Until 1863, the circuits were the Northern, the Home (which included the area around London), the Western, the Oxford, the Midland, the Norfolk, and the districts of North and South Wales.

Let me see – the Home, the Midland, Oxford, and Western, – ay, we can all cross the country well enough to our several destinations. – Traverse, when do you begin at Abingdon?

TRAVERSE.

The day after tomorrow.   20

FLOWER.

That is commission-day with us at Warwick, too. – But my clerk has retainers for every cause in the paper, so it will be time enough if I am there the next morning. – Besides, I have about half a dozen cases that have lain by me ever since the spring assizes, and I must tack opinions to them before I see   25 my country-clients again – so I will take the evening before me – and then *currente calamo*, as I say – eh, Traverse!

TRAVERSE.

True, Mr. Serjeant.

FLOWER.

Do you expect to have much to do on the Home circuit these assizes?   30

TRAVERSE.

Not much *nisi prius* business, but a good deal on the crown side, I believe. – The gaols are brimfull – and some of the felons in good circumstances and likely to be tolerable clients. – Let me see. I am engaged for three highway robberies, two murders, one forgery, and half a dozen larcenies, at Kingston.   35

FLOWER.

A pretty decent gaol delivery! – Do you expect to bring off Darkin, for the robbery on Putney-Common? Can you make out your *alibi*?

TRAVERSE.

Oh, no! the crown witnesses are sure to prove our identity. We shall certainly be hanged: but that don't signify. – But, Mr.   40

---

27 *currente calamo*] "With a running pen."

31 *nisi prius*] A term for a trial held outside London attended by one judge and a jury. Usually, High Court trials involved several judges. Here Traverse seems to mean "civil suits."

32 *gaols*] Spelled "goals" in early editions. The modern variant has been adopted here for the sake of clarity.

Serjeant, have you much to do? – Any remarkable cause on the Midland this circuit?

FLOWER.

Nothing very remarkable, – except two rapes, and Rider and Western at Nottingham, for *crim. con.* – but on the whole, I believe, a good deal of business. – Our associate tells me, that   45
there are above thirty *venires* for Warwick.

TRAVERSE.

Pray, Mr. Serjeant, are you concerned in Jones and Thomas at Lincoln?

FLOWER.

I am – for the plaintiff.

TRAVERSE.

And what do you think on't?   50

FLOWER.

A nonsuit.

TRAVERSE.

I thought so.

FLOWER.

Oh, no manner of doubt on't – *luce clarius* – we have no right in us – we have but one chance.

TRAVERSE.

What's that?   55

FLOWER.

Why, my Lord Chief does not go the circuit this time, and my brother Puzzle being in the commission, the cause will come on before him.

TRUEMAN.

Ay, that may do indeed, if you can but throw dust in the eyes of the defendant's council.   60

---

44 *crim. con.*] Short for "criminal conversation," i.e., adultery. Until 1857, husbands could obtain damages from the adulterer under this charge.

46 *venires*] Summonses.

51 nonsuit] A termination of an action where the plaintiff is unable to prove his case. Before 1875, plaintiffs could use this ruling to bring the same charges against the defendant, provided that that plaintiff had paid all costs from the previous trial.

53 *luce clarius*] "By the clear light of day."

FLOWER.

True. – [*To* Trueman.] Mr. Trueman, I think you are concerned for Lord Ogleby in this affair?

TRUEMAN.

I am, Sir – I have the honour to be related to his Lordship, and hold some courts for him in Somersetshire, – go the Western circuit – and attend the sessions at Exeter, merely   65
because his Lordship's interest and property lie in that part of the kingdom.

FLOWER.

Ha! – and pray, Mr. Trueman, how long have you been called to the bar?

TRUEMAN.

About nine years and three quarters.   70

FLOWER.

Ha! – I don't know that I ever had the pleasure of seeing you before. – I wish you success, young gentleman!

Enter Sterling.

STERLING.

Oh, Mr. Serjeant Flower, I am glad to see you. – Your servant, Mr. Serjeant! Gentlemen, your servant! – Well, are all matters concluded? Has the snail-paced conveyancer, old Ferret of   75
Gray's Inn, settled the articles at last? Do you approve of what he has done? Will his tackle hold? tight and strong? – Eh, master Serjeant?

FLOWER.

My friend Ferret's slow and sure, Sir. – But then, *serius aut citius*, as we say, – sooner or later, Mr. Sterling, he is sure to put   80
his business out of hand as he should do. – My clerk has brought the writings, and all other instruments along with him, and the settlement is, I believe, as good a settlement as any settlement on the face of the earth!

79-80 *serius aut citius*] "Sooner or later."

STERLING.

> But that damned mortgage of 60,000 l. – There don't appear   85
> to be any other incumbrances, I hope?

TRAVERSE.

> I can answer for that, Sir – and that will be cleared off imme-
> diately on the payment of the first part of Miss Sterling's por-
> tion. – You agree, on your part, to come down with 80,000 l. –

STERLING.

> Down on the nail. – Ay, ay, my money is ready tomorrow if
> he pleases – he shall have it in India-bonds, or notes, or how   90
> he chuses. – Your lords, and your dukes, and your people at
> the court-end of town stick at payments sometimes – debts
> unpaid, no credit left with them – but no fear of us substan-
> tial fellows – eh, Mr. Serjeant! –

FLOWER.   95

> Sir John, having last term, according to agreement, levied a
> fine, and suffered a recovery, has thereby cut off the entail of
> the Ogleby estate for the better effecting the purposes of the
> present intended marriage; on which above-mentioned
> Ogleby estate, a jointure of 2000 l. per ann. is secured to your
> eldest daughter, now Elizabeth Sterling, spinster, and the   100
> whole estate, after the death of the aforesaid Earl, descends to
> the heirs male of Sir John Melvil on the body of the aforesaid
> Elizabeth Sterling lawfully to be begotten.

TRAVERSE.

> Very true – and Sir John is to be put in immediate possession
> of as much of his Lordship's Somersetshire estate, as lies in the   105
> manors of Hogmore and Cranford, amounting to between
> two and three thousands per ann. and at the death of Mr.
> Sterling, a further sum of seventy thousand –

Enter Sir John Melvil.

STERLING.

> Ah, Sir John! Here we are – hard at it – paving the road to
> matrimony. – We'll have no jolts; all upon the nail, as easy as   110
> the new pavement. – First the lawyers, then comes the doc-
> tor. – Let us but dispatch the long-robe, we shall soon set
> Pudding-sleeves to work, I warrant you.

SIR JOHN.

I am sorry to interrupt you, Sir – but I hope that both you   115
and these gentlemen will excuse me – having something very
particular for your private ear, I took the liberty of following
you, and beg you will oblige me with an audience immediately.

STERLING.

Ay, with all my heart. – Gentlemen, Mr. Serjeant, you'll ex-   120
cuse it. – Business must be done, you know. – The writings
will keep cold till tomorrow morning.

FLOWER.

I must be at Warwick, Mr. Sterling, the day after.

STERLING.

Nay, nay, I shan't part with you tonight, gentlemen, I promise
you. – My house is very full, but I have beds for you all, beds   125
for your servants, and stabling for all your horses. – Will you
take a turn in the garden, and view some of my improvements before dinner? Or will you amuse yourselves in the
green, with a game of bowls and a cool tankard? – My servants shall attend you. – Do you chuse any other refresh-   130
ment? – Call for what you please; – do as you please; – make
yourselves quite at home, I beg of you. – Here, – Thomas,
Harry, William, wait on these Gentlemen! [*Follows the lawyers out, bawling and talking, and then returns to* Sir John.] And
now, Sir, I am entirely at your service. – What are your com-   135
mands with me, Sir John?

SIR JOHN.

After having carried the negotiation between our families to
so great a length, after having assented so readily to all your
proposals, as well as received so many instances of your chearful compliance with the demands made on our part, I am ex-   140
tremely concerned, Mr. Sterling, to be the involuntary cause
of any uneasiness.

STERLING.

Uneasiness! what uneasiness? – Where business is transacted
as it ought to be, and the parties understand one another,
there can be no uneasiness. You agree, on such and such con-   145
ditions to receive my daughter for a wife; on the same conditions I agree to receive you as a son-in-law; and as to all the

rest, it follows of course, you know, as regularly as the payment of a bill after acceptance.

SIR JOHN.

Pardon me, Sir; more uneasiness has arisen than you are aware   150
of. I am myself, at this instant, in a state of inexpressible embarrassment; Miss Sterling, I know, is extremely disconcerted too; and unless you will oblige me with the assistance of your friendship, I foresee the speedy progress of discontent and animosity through the whole family.   155

STERLING.

What the deuce is all this? I don't understand a single syllable.

SIR JOHN.

In one word, then – it will be absolutely impossible for me to fulfill my engagement in regard to Miss Sterling.

STERLING.

How, Sir John? Do you mean to put an affront upon my family? What! refuse to –   160

SIR JOHN.

Be assured, Sir, that I neither mean to affront, nor forsake your family. – My only fear is, that you should desert me; for the whole happiness of my life depends on being connected with your family by the nearest and tenderest ties in the world.   165

STERLING.

Why, did you not tell me, but a moment ago, that it was absolutely impossible for you to marry my daughter?

SIR JOHN.

True. – But you have another daughter, Sir –

STERLING.

Well?

SIR JOHN.

Who has obtained the most absolute dominion over my   170
heart. I have already declared my passion to her; nay, Miss Sterling herself is also apprized of it, and if you will but give a sanction to my present addresses, the uncommon merit of Miss Sterling will no doubt recommend her to a person of equal, if not superior rank to myself, and our families may   175
still be allied by my union with Miss Fanny.

STERLING.

> Mighty fine, truly! Why, what the plague do you make of us,
> Sir John? Do you come to market for my daughters, like ser-
> vants at a statute-fair? Do you think that I will suffer you, or
> any man in the world, to come into my house, like the Grand   180
> Signior, and throw the handkerchief first to one, and then to
> t'other, just as he pleases? Do you think that I drive a kind of
> African slave trade with them? and –

SIR JOHN.

> A moment's patience, Sir! Nothing but the excess of my pas-
> sion for Miss Fanny should have induced me to take any step   185
> that had the least appearance of disrespect to any part of your
> family; and even now I am desirous to atone for my trans-
> gression, by making the most adequate compensation that
> lies in my power.

STERLING.

> Compensation! What compensation can you possibly make   190
> in such a case as this, Sir John?

SIR JOHN.

> Come, come, Mr. Sterling; I know you to be a man of sense, a
> man of business, a man of the world. I'll deal frankly with
> you; and you shall see that I do not desire a change of meas-
> ures for my own gratification, without endeavouring to make   195
> it advantageous to you.

STERLING.

> What advantage can your inconstancy be to me, Sir John?

SIR JOHN.

> I'll tell you, Sir. – You know that by the articles at present
> subsisting between us, on the day of my marriage with Miss
> Sterling, you agree to pay down the gross sum of eighty   200
> thousand pounds.

STERLING.

> Well!

SIR JOHN.

> Now if you will but consent to my waving that marriage –

STERLING.

> I agree to your waving that marriage? Impossible, Sir John!

SIR JOHN.

I hope not, Sir; as on my part, I will agree to wave my right to   205
thirty thousand pounds of the fortune I was to receive with
her.

STERLING.

Thirty thousand, d'ye say?

SIR JOHN.

Yes, Sir; and accept of Miss Fanny with fifty thousand, instead
of fourscore.   210

STERLING.

Fifty thousand – [Pausing.]

SIR JOHN.

Instead of fourscore.

STERLING.

Why, – why, – there may be something in that. – Let me see; –
Fanny with fifty thousand instead of Betsey with fourscore. –
But how can this be, Sir John? – For you know that I am to   215
pay this money into the hands of my Lord Ogleby; who, I believe – between you and me, Sir John, – is not overstocked
with ready money at present; and threescore thousand of it,
you know, is to go to pay off the present incumbrances on the
estate, Sir John.   220

SIR JOHN.

That objection is easily obviated. – Ten thousand of the
twenty thouand, which would remain as a surplus of the
fourscore, after paying off the mortgage, was intended by his
Lordship for my use, that we might set off with some little
éclat on our marriage; and the other ten for his own. – Ten   225
thousand pounds therefore I shall be able to pay you immediately; and for the remaining twenty thousand you shall have a
mortgage on that part of the estate which is to be made over
to me, with whatever security you shall require for the regular payment of the interest, 'till the principal is duly dis-   230
charged.

STERLING.

Why – to do you justice, Sir John, there is something fair and
open in your proposal; and since I find you do not mean to
put an affront upon the family –

SIR JOHN.

Nothing was ever farther from my thoughts, Mr. Sterling. –   235
And after all, the whole affair is nothing extraordinary – such
things happen every day – and as the world has only heard
generally of a treaty between the families, when this marriage
takes place, nobody will be the wiser, if we have but discretion enough to keep our own counsel.   240

STERLING.

True, true; and since you only transfer from one girl to the
other, it is no more than transferring so much stock, you
know.

SIR JOHN.

The very thing.

STERLING.

Odso! I had quite forgot. We are reckoning without our host   245
here. There is another difficulty –

SIR JOHN.

You alarm me. What can that be?

STERLING.

I can't stir a step in this business without consulting my sister
Heidelberg. – The family has very great expectations from
her, and we must not give her any offense.   250

SIR JOHN.

But if you come into this measure, surely she will be so kind
as to consent –

STERLING.

I don't know that – Betsey is her darling, and I can't tell how
far she may resent any slight that seems to be offered to her
favourite niece. – However, I'll do the best I can for you. –   255
You shall go and break the matter to her first, and by that
time that I may suppose that your rhetorick has prevailed on
her to listen to reason, I will step in to reinforce your argu-
ments.

SIR JOHN.

I'll fly to her immediately: you promise me your assistance?   260

STERLING.

I do.

SIR JOHN.

Ten thousand thanks for it! and now success attend me! [*Going.*]

STERLING.

    Harkee, Sir John!

                Sir John *returns.*

STERLING.

    Not a word of the thirty thousand to my sister, Sir John.

SIR JOHN.

    Oh, I am dumb, I am dumb, Sir. [*Going.*]   265

STERLING.

    You remember it is thirty thousand.

SIR JOHN.

    To be sure I do. [*Going.*]

STERLING.

    But Sir John! – one thing more. [Sir John *returns.*] My Lord
    must know nothing of this stroke of friendship between us.

SIR JOHN.

    Not for the world. – Let me alone! Let me alone! [*Offering to*   270
    go.]

STERLING [*Holding him*].

    – And when every thing is agreed, we must give each other a
    bond to be held fast to the bargain.

SIR JOHN.

    To be sure. A bond by all means! A bond, or whatever you
    please.

                Exit hastily.

STERLING [*alone*].

    I should have thought of more conditions – he's in a humour   275
    to give me everything. – Why, what mere children are your
    fellows of quality; that cry for a plaything one minute, and
    throw it by the next! As changeable as the weather, and as un-
    certain as the stocks. – Special fellows to drive a bargain! and
    yet they are to take care of the interest of the nation truly! –   280
    Here does this whirligig man of fashion offer to give up
    thirty thousand pounds in hard money, with as much indif-
    ference as if it was a china orange. – By this mortgage, I shall
    have a hold on his *Terra-firma*, and if he wants more money, as
    he certainly will, – let him have children by my daughter or   285

no, I shall have his whole estate in a net for the benefit of my
family. − Well; thus it is, that the children of citizens, who
have acquired fortunes, prove persons of fashion; and thus it is
that persons of fashion, who have ruined their fortunes, re-
duce the next generation to cits.   290

Exit.

SCENE *changes to another apartment.*   [III.ii
Enter Mrs. Heidelberg, *and* Miss Sterling.

MISS STERLING.

This is your gentle-looking, soft-speaking, sweet-smiling, af-
fable Miss Fanny for you!

MRS. HEIDELBERG.

My Miss Fanny! I disclaim her. With all her arts she never
could insinuat herself into my good graces − and yet she has a
way with her, that deceives man, woman, and child, except   5
you and me, niece.

MISS STERLING.

O ay; she wants nothing but a crook in her hand, and a lamb
under her arm, to be a perfect picture of innocence and simplicity.

MRS. HEIDELBERG.

Just as I was drawn at Amsterdam, when I went over to visit   10
my husband's relations.

MISS STERLING.

And then she's so mighty good to servants − *pray, John, do this*
− *pray, Tom, do that* − *thank you, Jenny* − and then so humble to
her relations − *to be sure, Papa! − as my Aunt pleases − my Sister
knows best.* − But with all her demureness and humility she   15
has no objection to be Lady Melvil, it seems, nor to any
wickedness that can make her so.

MRS. HEIDELBERG.

She Lady Melville? Compose yourself, Niece! I'll ladyship
her, indeed: − a little creepin, cantin. − She shan't be the better for a farden of my money. But tell me, child, how does this 20
intriguing with Sir John correspond with her partiality to
Lovewell? I don't see a concatunation here.

MISS STERLING.

There I was deceived, Madam. I took all their whisperings
and stealing into corners to be the mere attraction of vulgar
minds; but behold! their private meetings were not to con-   25
trive their own insipid happiness, but to conspire against
mine. – But I know whence proceeds Mr. Lovewell's resentment to me. I could not stoop to be familiar with my father's
clerk, and so I have lost his interest.

MRS. HEIDELBER.

My spurrit to a T. – My dear child! [*Kissing her.*] – Mr.   30
Heidelberg lost his election for a member of parliament, because I would not demean myself to be slobbered about by
drunken shoemakers, beastly cheesemongers, and greasy
butchers and tallow-chandlers. However, Niece, I can't help
diffuring a little in opinon from you in this matter. My expe-   35
runce and sagucity makes me still suspect, that there is something more between her and that Lovewell, notwithstanding
this affair of Sir John. – I had my eye upon them the whole
time of breakfast. – Sir John, I observed, looked a little confounded, indeed, though I knew nothing of what had passed   40
in the garden. You seemed to sit upon thorns, too: but Fanny
and Mr. Lovewell made quite another-guess sort of figur; and
were as perfet a pictur of two distrest lovers, as if it had been
drawn by Raphael Angelo. – As to Sir John and Fanny, I want
a matter of fact.   45

MISS STERLING.

Matter of fact, Madam! Did not I come unexpectedly upon
them? Was not Sir John kneeling at her feet, and kissing her
hand? Did not he look all love, and she all confusion? Is not
that matter of fact? And did not Sir John, the moment that
Papa was called out of the room to the lawyer-men, get up   50
from breakfast, and follow him immediately? And I warrant
you that by this time he has made proposals to him to marry
my sister. – Oh, that some other person, an earl, or a duke,
would make his address to me, that I might be revenged on
this monster!   55

MRS. HEIDELBERG.

Be cool, child! You *shall* be Lady Melvil, in spite of all their
caballins, if it costs me ten thousand pounds to turn the scale.

Sir John may apply to my brother, indeed; but I'll make them all know who governs in this fammaly.

MISS STERLING.

As I live, Madam, yonder comes Sir John. A base man! I can't   60
endure the sight of him. I'll leave the room this instant. [*Disordered.*]

MRS. HEIDELBERG.

Poor thing! Well, retire to your own chamber, child; I'll give it him, I warrant you; and by and by I'll come, and let you know all that has past between us.

MISS STERLING.

Pray do, Madam! – [*Looking back.*] – A vile wretch!   65

Exit in a rage.
Enter Sir John Melvil.

SIR JOHN.

Your most humble obedient servant, Madam! [*Bowing very respectably.*]

MRS. HEIDELBERG.

Your servant, Sir John! [*Dropping a half-curtsy, then pouting.*]

SIR JOHN.

Miss Sterling's manner of quitting the room on my approach, and the visible coolness of your behaviour to me, Madam, convince me that she has acquainted you with what past this   70
morning.

MRS. HEIDELBERG.

I am very sorry, Sir John, to be made acquainted with any thing that should induce me to change the opinon, which I could always wish to entertain of a person of quallaty. [*Pouting.*]

SIR JOHN.

It has always been my ambition to merit the best opinion   75
from Mrs. Heidelberg; and when she comes to weigh all circumstances, I flatter myself –

MRS. HEIDELBERG.

You *do* flatter yourself, if you imagine that I can approve your behaviour to my niece, Sir John. – And give me leave to tell you, Sir John, that you have been drawn into an action much   80
beneath you, Sir John; and that I look upon every injury of-

fered to Miss Betty Sterling, as an affront to myself, Sir John. [*Warmly.*]

SIR JOHN.

I would not offend you for the world, Madam! But when I am influenced by a partiality for another, however ill-founded, I hope your discernment and good sense will think   85
it rather a point of honour to renounce engagements, which I could not fulfil so strictly as I ought; and that you will ex-cuse the change in my inclinations, since the new object, as well as the first, has the honour of being your niece, Madam.

MRS. HEIDELBERG.

I disclaim her as a niece, Sir John; Miss Sterling disclaims her   90
as a sister, and the whole fammaly must disclaim her, for her monstrous baseness and treachery.

SIR JOHN.

Indeed she has been guilty of none, Madam. Her hand and heart are, I am sure, entirely at the disposal of yourself and Mr. Sterling.   95

Enter Sterling *behind.*

And if you should not oppose my inclinations, I am sure of Mr. Sterling's consent, Madam.

MRS. HEIDELBERG.

Indeed!

SIR JOHN.

Quite certain, Madam.

STERLING [*Behind*].

So! they seem to be coming to terms already. I may venture   100
to make my appearance.

MRS. HEIDELBERG.

To marry Fanny? [Sterling *advances by degrees.*]

SIR JOHN.

Yes, Madam.

MRS. HEIDELBERG.

My brother has given his consent, you say?

SIR JOHN.

In the most ample manner, with no other restriction than the   105
failure of your concurrence, Madam. – [*Sees* Sterling.] – Oh, here's Mr. Sterling, who will confirm what I have told you.

MRS. HEIDELBERG.

What! Have you consented to give up your own daughter in
this manner, brother?

STERLING.

Give her up! no, not give her up, sister; only in case that you –   110
[*Apart to* Sir John.] Zounds, I am afraid you have said too
much, Sir John.

MRS. HEIDELBERG.

Yes, yes. I see now that it is true enough what my niece told
me. You are all plottin and caballin against her. – Pray, does
Lord Ogleby know of this affair?   115

SIR JOHN.

I have not yet made him acquainted with it, Madam.

MRS. HEIDELBERG.

No, I warrant you. I thought so. – And so his Lordship and
myself truly, are not to be consulted 'till the last.

STERLING.

What! did you not consult my Lord? Oh, fie for shame, Sir
John!   120

SIR JOHN.

Nay, but Mr. Sterling –

MRS. HEIDELBERG.

We, who are the persons of most consequence and expe-
runce in the two fammalies, are to know nothing of the matter, 'till the whole is as good as concluded upon. But his
Lordship, I am sure, will have more generosaty than to coun-   125
tenance for such a perceeding. – And I could not have expected such a behaviour from a person of your quallaty, Sir
John. – And as for you, brother –

STERLING.

Nay, nay, but hear me, sister!

MRS. HEIDELBERG.

I am perfetly ashamed of you. – Have you no spurrit? No   130
more concern for the honour of our fammaly than to consent –

STERLING.

Consent? – I consent! – As I hope for mercy, I never gave my
consent. Did I consent, Sir John?

SIR JOHN.

Not absolutely, without Mrs. Heidelberg's concurrence. But   135
in case of her approbation –

STERLING.

Ay, I grant you, if my sister approved. – [*To* Mrs. Heidelberg.]
But that's quite another thing, you know.

MRS. HEIDELBERG.

Your sister, approve, indeed! – I thought you knew her better,
brother Sterling! – What! approve of having your eldest   140
daughter returned upon our hands, and exchanged for the
younger? – I am surprized how you could listen to such a
scandalus proposal.

STERLING.

I tell you, I never did listen to it. – Did not I say that I would
be governed entirely by my sister, Sir John? – And unless she   145
agreed to your marrying Fanny –

MRS. HEIDELBERG.

I agree to his marrying Fanny? Abominable! The man is absolutely out of his senses. – Can't that wise head of yours
foresee the consequence of all this, brother Sterling? Will Sir
John take Fanny without a fortune? No. – After you have set-   150
tled the largest part of your property on your youngest
daughter, can there be an equal portion left for the eldest?
No. – Does this not overturn the whole systum of the fammaly? Yes, yes, yes. You know I was always for my niece Betsey's marrying a person of the very first quallaty. That was my   155
maxum. And, therefore, much the largest settlement was of
course to be made upon her. – As for Fanny, if she could, with
the fortune of twenty or thirty thousand pounds, get a
knight, or a member of parliament, or a rich common-coun-
cil-man for a husband, I thought it might do very well.   160

SIR JOHN.

But if a better match should offer itself, why should not it be
accepted, Madam?

159-60 common-council-man] A Councillor of the City of London.

MRS. HEIDELBERG.

What! at the expence of her elder sister! Oh fie, Sir John! –
How could you bear to hear of such an indignaty, brother
Sterling?   165

STERLING.

I! Nay, I shan't hear of it, I promise you. – I can't hear of it indeed, Sir John.

MRS. HEIDELBERG.

But you *have* heard of it, brother Sterling. You know you
have; and sent Sir John to propose it to me. But if you can
give up your daughter, I shan't forsake my niece, I assure you.   170
Ah! if my poor dear Mr. Heidelberg, and our own sweet
babes had been alive, he would not have behaved so.

STERLING.

Did I, Sir John? Nay, speak! – [*Apart to* Sir John.] Bring me
off, or we are ruined.

SIR JOHN.

Why, to be sure, to speak the truth –   175

MRS. HEIDELBERG.

To speak the truth, I'm ashamed of you both. But have a care
what you are about, brother! have a care, I say. The lawyers are
in the house, I hear; and if everything is not settled to my lik-
ing, I'll have nothing more to say to you, if I live these hundred years. – I'll go over to Holland, and settle with Mr. Van-   180
derspracken, my poor husband's first cousin; and my own
fammaly shall never be the better for a farden of my money, I
promise you.

Exit.
Manent Sir John, *and* Sterling.

STERLING.

I thought so. I knew she never would agree to it.

SIR JOHN.

'Sdeath, how unfortunate! What can we do, Mr. Sterling?   185

STERLING.

Nothing.

SIR JOHN.

What! must our agreement break off, the moment it is made
then?

STERLING.

It can't be helped, Sir John. The family, as I told you before, have great expectations from my sister; and if this matter pro- 190 ceeds, you hear yourself that she threatens to leave us. – My brother Heidelberg was a warm man; a very warm man; and died worth a Plumb at least; a Plumb! Ay, I warrant you, he died worth a Plumb and a half.

SIR JOHN.

Well; but if I – 195

STERLING.

And then, my sister has three or four very good mortgages, a deal of money in the three per cents, and old South Sea annuities, besides large concerns in the Dutch and French funds. – The greatest part of all this she means to leave to our family. 200

SIR JOHN.

I can only say, Sir –

STERLING.

Why, your offer of the difference of thirty thousand, was very fair and handsome to be sure, Sir John.

SIR JOHN.

Nay, but I am even willing to –

STERLING.

Ay, but if I was willing to accept it against her will, I might 205 lose above a hundred thousand; so, you see, the ballance is against you, Sir John.

SIR JOHN.

But is there no way, do you think, of prevailing on Mrs. Heidelberg to grant her consent?

STERLING.

I am afraid not. – However, when her passion is a little abated 210 – for she's very passionate – you may try what can be done: but you must not use my name any more, Sir John.

---

192 warm] Business slang term for "rich," but also, according to Johnson, "busy, zealous, active."

193 Plumb] Also "plum." Business slang for £100,000.

SIR JOHN.

Suppose I was to prevail on Lord Ogleby to apply to her, do
you think that would have any influence over her?

STERLING.

I think he would be more likely to persuade her to it, than   215
any other person in the family. She has a great respect for
Lord Ogleby. She loves a lord.

SIR JOHN.

I'll apply to him this very day. – And if he should prevail on
Mrs. Heidelberg, I may depend on your friendship, Mr. Sterling?   220

STERLING.

Ay, ay, I shall be glad to oblige you, when it is in my power;
but as the account stands now, you see it is not upon the figures. And so your servant, Sir John.

Exit.

SIR JOHN [*Alone*].

What a situation am I in! – Breaking off with her whom I
was bound by treaty to marry; rejected by the object of my   225
affections; and embroiled with this turbulent woman, who
governs the whole family. – And yet opposition, instead of
smothering, increases my inclination. I must have her. I'll apply immediately to Lord Ogleby; and if he can but bring over
the aunt to our party, her influence will overcome the scru-   230
ples and delicacy of my dear Fanny, and I shall be the happiest
of mankind.

Exit.

ACT IV

SCENE 1, *A room.*   [IV.i]

Enter Sterling, Mrs. Heidelberg, *and* Miss Sterling.

STERLING.

What! will you send Fanny to town, sister?

MRS. HEIDELBERG.

Tomorrow morning. I've given orders about it already.

STERLING.

Indeed?

MRS. HEIDELBERG.

Positively.

STERLING.

But consider, sister, at such a time as this, what an odd ap-   5
pearance it will have.

MRS. HEIDELBERG.

Not half as odd as her behaviour, brother. – This time was intended for happiness, and I'll keep no incendiaries here to
destroy it. I insist on her going off tomorrow morning.

STERLING.

I'm afraid all this is your doing, Betsey.   10

MISS STERLING.

No indeed, Papa. My aunt knows that it is not. – For all
Fanny's baseness to me, I am sure that I would not do, or say
anything to hurt her with you or my aunt for the world.

MRS. HEIDELBERG.

Hold your tongue, Betsey! – I will have my way. – When she
is packed off, every thing will go on as it should do. – Since   15
they are at their intrigues, I'll let them see that we can act
with vigur on our part; and the sending her out of the way
shall be the purliminary step to all the rest of my perceedings.

STERLING.

Well, but sister –

MRS. HEIDELBERG.

It does not signify talking, brother Sterling, for I'm resolved   20
to be rid of her, and I will. – [*To* Miss Sterling.]. Come along,
child! – The post-shay shall be at the door by six o'clock in
the morning; and if Miss Fanny does not get into it, why *I*
will, and so there's an end of the matter.

THE CLANDESTINE MARRIAGE   113

Bounces out with Miss Sterling.
Mrs. Heidelberg *returns.*

One more word, brother Sterling! I expect that you will take   25
your eldest daughter in your hand, and make a formal com-
plaint to Lord Ogleby of Sir John Melvil's behaviour. – Do
this, brother; shew a proper regard for the honour of your
fammaly yourself, and I shall throw in my mite to the raising
of it. If not – but now you know my mind. So act as you   30
please, and take the consequences.

Exit.

STERLING [*Alone*].

The devil's in the woman for tyranny – mothers, wives, mistresses, or sisters, they always will govern us. – As to my sister
Heidelberg, she knows the strength of her purse, and domi-
neers upon the credit of it. – [*Mimicking.*] "I will do this" –   35
and "you shall do that" – and "you must do t'other, or else
the fammaly shan't have a farden of." – So absolute with her
money! – But to say the truth, nothing but money *can* make
us absolute, and so we must e'en make the best of her.

S C E N E *changes to the garden.*   [IV.ii]
Enter Lord Ogleby *and* Canton.

LORD OGLEBY.

What! Mademoiselle Fanny to be sent away! – Why? –
Wherefore? – What's the meaning of all this?

CANTON.

Je ne scais pas. – I know noting of it.

LORD OGLEBY.

It can't be; it shan't be. I protest against the measure. She's a
fine girl, and I had much rather that the rest of the family   5
were annihilated than that she should leave us. – Her vulgar
father, that's the very abstract of 'Change-Alley – the aunt,
that's always endeavouring to be a fine lady – and the pert sister, for ever shewing that she is one, are horrid company in-

deed, and without her would be intolerable. Ah, la petite 10
Fanchon! She's the thing. Isn't she, Cant?

CANTON.

Dere is very good sympatie entre vous, and dat young lady,
mi Lor.

LORD OGLEBY.

I'll not be left among these Goths and Vandals, your Sterlings,
your Heidelbergs, and Devilbergs. – If she goes, I'll positively 15
go too.

CANTON.

In de same post-chay, mi Lor? You have no object to dat, I believe, nor Mademoiselle neider, too – ha, ha. ha.

LORD OGLEBY.

Prithee hold thy foolish tongue, Cant. Does thy Swiss stupidity imagine that I can see and talk with a fine girl without 20
desires? – My eyes are involuntarily attracted to beautiful objects – I fly as naturally to a fine girl –

CANTON.

As de fine girl fly to you, my Lor, ha, ha ha; you always fly to-
gedre like un pair de pigeons. –

LORD OGLEBY [*Mocks him*].

Like un pair de pigeons. – Vous etes un sot, Mons. Canton – 25
Thou art always dreaming of my intrigues, and never seest
me *badiner*, but you suspect mischief, you old fool, you.

CANTON.

I am fool, I confess, but not always fool in dat, my Lor. he, he,
he.

LORD OGLEBY.

He, he, he. Thou art incorrigble, but thy absurdities amuse 30
one. – Thou art like my rapee here, [*Takes out his box.*] a most
ridiculous superfluity, but a pinch of thee now and then is a
most delicious treat.

CANTON.

You do me great honeur, my Lor.

---

27 *badiner*] to jest.
31 rapee] "A coarse kind of snuff made from darker and ranker tobacco-leaves,
and originally obtained by rasping a piece of tobacco" (OED).

LORD OGLEBY.

'Tis fact, upon my soul. – Thou art properly my cephalick   35
snuff, and art no bad medicine against megrims, vertigoes,
and profound thinking – ha, ha, ha.

CANTON.

Your flatterie, my Lor, vil make me too prode.

LORD OGLEBY.

The girl has some little partiality for me, to be sure: but
prithee, Cant, is not that Miss Fanny yonder?   40

CANTON [*Looking with a glass*].

En veritè, 'tis she, my Lor – 'tis one of de pigeons, – de pigeons d'amour.

LORD OGLEBY [*Smiling*].

Don't be ridiculous, you old monkey.

CANTON.

I am monkeè, I am ole, but I have eye, I have ear, and a little
understand, now and den. –   45

LORD OGLEBY.

Taisez vous bête!

CANTON.

Elle vous attend, my Lor. – She vil make a love to you.

LORD OGLEBY.

Will she? Have at her, then! A fine girl can't oblige me more.
– Egad, I find myself a little enjouée – come along, Cant! She
is but in the next walk – but there is such deal of this damned   50
crinkum-crankum, as Sterling calls it, that one sees people for
half an hour before one can get to them. – Allons, Mons.
Canton, allons donc!

Exeunt singing in French.

Another part of the garden.
Lovewell, *and* Fanny.

---

36 megrims] This word is the ancestor of our present-day "migraines"; in
eighteenth-century use, however, the word simply referred to any nervous
disorder.

LOVEWELL.

My dear Fanny, I cannot bear your distress; it overcomes all
my resolutions, and I am prepared for the discovery. 55

FANNY.

But how can it be effected before my departure?

LOVEWELL.

I'll tell you. – Lord Ogleby seems to entertain a visible partiality for you; and notwithstanding the peculiarities of his behaviour, I am sure that he is humane at the bottom. He is vain
to an excess; but withall extremely good-natured, and would 60
do any thing to recommend himself to a lady. – Do you open
the whole affair of our marriage to him immediately. It will
come with more irresistible persuasion from you than from
myself; and I doubt not but you'll gain his friendship and
protection at once. – His influence and authority will put an 65
end to Sir John's sollicitations, remove your aunt's and sister's
unkindness and suspicions, and, I hope, reconcile your father
and the whole family to our marriage.

FANNY.

Heaven grant it! Where is my Lord?

LOVEWELL.

I have heard him and Canton since dinner singing French 70
songs under the great walnut-tree by the parlour door. If you
meet with him in the garden, you may disclose the whole
immediately.

FANNY.

Dreadful as the task is, I'll do it. – Any thing is better than this
continual anxiety. 75

LOVEWELL.

By that time the discovery is made, I will appear to second
you. – Ha! here comes my Lord. – Now, my dear Fanny, sum-
mon up all your spirits, plead our cause powerfully, and be
sure of success. –

Going.

FANNY.

Ah, don't leave me! 80

LOVEWELL.

Nay, you must let me.

FANNY.

Well; since it must be so, I'll obey you, if I have the power. Oh Lovewell!

LOVEWELL.

Consider, our situation is very critical. Tomorrow morning is fixt for your departure, and if we lose this opportunity, we may wish in vain for another. – He approaches – I must retire. – Speak, my dear Fanny, speak, and make us happy! 85

Exit.

FANNY [*Alone*].

Good heaven, what a situation am I in! What shall I do? What shall I say to him? I am all confusion.

Enter Lord Ogleby and Canton.

LORD OGLEBY.

To see such beauty so solitary, Madam, is a satire upon mankind, and 'tis fortunate that one man has broke in upon your reverie for the credit of our sex. – I say *one*, Madam, for poor Canton here, from age and infirmities, stands for nothing. 90

CANTON.

Noting at all, inteed.

FANNY.

Your Lordship does me great honour. – I had a favour to request, my Lord! 95

LORD OGLEBY.

A favour, Madam! – To be honoured with your commands, is an inexpressible favour done to me, Madam.

FANNY.

If your Lordship could indulge me with the honour of a moment's. – [*Aside.*] What is the matter with me? 100

LORD OGLEBY [*To* Canton].

The girl's confused – he! – here's something in the wind, faith – I'll have a tete-a-tete with her – allez vous en!

CANTON.

I go – ah, pauvre Mademoiselle! My Lor, have *pitié* upon the poor *pigeone*!

LORD OGLEBY [*Smiling*].

I'll knock you down, Cant, if you're impertinent.   105

CANTON.

Den I mus avay – [*Shuffles along.*] [*Aside.*] – You are mosh
please, for all dat.

Exit.

FANNY [*Aside*].

I shall sink with apprehension.

LORD OGLEBY.

What a sweet girl! – She's a civilized being, and atones for the
barbarism of the rest of the family.   110

FANNY.

My Lord! I – [*She curtseys, and blushes.*]

LORD OGLEBY [*Addressing her*].

I look upon it, Madam, to be one of the luckiest circumstances of my life, that I have this moment the honour of receiving your commands, and the satisfaction of confirming
with my tongue, what my eyes perhaps have too weakly ex-   115
pressed – that I am literally – the humblest of your servants.

FANNY.

I think myself greatly honoured, by your Lordship's partiality
to me; but it distresses me, that I am obliged in my present
situation to apply to it for protection.

LORD OGLEBY.

I am happy in your distress, Madam, because it gives me an   120
opportunity to shew my zeal. Beauty to me, is a religion, in
which I was born and bred a bigot, and would die a martyr. –
[*Aside.*] I'm in tolerable spirits, faith!

FANNY.

There is not perhaps at this moment a more distressed creature than myself. Affection, duty, hope, despair, and a thou-   125
sand different sentiments, are struggling in my bosom; and
even the presence of your Lordship, to whom I have flown
for protection, adds to my perplexity.

LORD OGLEBY.

Does it, Madam? – Venus forbid! – [*Aside and smiling.*] My old
fault; the devil's in me, I think, for perplexing young women.   130
[*Aloud.*] Take courage, Madam! Dear Miss Fanny, explain. –

You have a powerful advocate in my breast, I assure you – my heart, Madam – I am attached to you by all the laws of sympathy, and delicacy. – By my honour, I am.

FANNY.

Then I will venture to unburthen my mind. – Sir John   135
Melvil, my Lord, by the most misplaced, and mistimed declaration of affection for me, has made me the most unhappiest of women.

LORD OGLEBY.

How, Madam! Has Sir John made his addresses to you?

FANNY.

He has, my Lord, in the strongest terms. But I hope it is need-   140
less to say, that my duty to my father, love to my sister, and regard to the whole family, as well as the great respect I entertain for your Lordship, [*Curtseying.*] made me shudder at his addresses.

LORD OGLEBY.

Charming girl! – Proceed, my dear Miss Fanny, proceed!   145

FANNY.

In a moment – give me leave, my Lord! – But if what I have to disclose should be received with anger or displeasure –

LORD OGLEBY.

Impossible, by all the tender powers! – Speak, I beseech you, or I shall divine the cause before you utter it.

FANNY.

Then, my Lord, Sir John's addresses are not only shocking to   150
me in themselves, but are more particularly disagreeable to me at this time, as – as – [*Hesitating.*]

LORD OGLEBY.

As what, Madam?

FANNY.

As – pardon my confusion – I am intirely devoted to another.

LORD OGLEBY [*Aside*].

If this is not plain, the devil's in it. – [*Aloud.*] But tell me, my   155
dear Miss Fanny, for I must know; tell me the how, the when, and the where. – Tell me –

Enter Canton *hastily.*

CANTON.

My Lor, my Lor, my Lor! –

LORD OGLEBY.

Damn your Swiss impertinence! How durst you interrupt
me in the most critical melting moment that ever love and   160
beauty honoured me with?

CANTON.

I demande pardonne, my Lor! Sir John Melvil, my Lor, sent
me to beg you to do him the honour to speak a little to your
Lorship.

LORD OGLEBY.

I'm not at leisure. – I'm busy. – Get away, you stupid old dog,   165
you Swiss rascal, or I'll –

CANTON.

Fort bien, my Lor. – [Canton *goes out tiptoe.*]

LORD OGLEBY.

By the laws of gallantry, Madam, this interruption should be
death; but as no punishment ought to disturb the triumph of
the softer passions, the criminal is pardoned and dismissed. –   170
Let us return, Madam, to the highest luxury of exalted minds
– a declaration of love from the lips of beauty.

FANNY.

The entrance of a third person has a little relieved me, but I
cannot go through with it – and yet I must open my heart
with a discovery, or it will break with its burthen.   175

LORD OGLEBY [*Aside*].

What passion in her eyes! I am alarmed to agitation. –
[*Aloud.*] I presume, Madam, (and as you have flattered me, by
making me a party concerned, I hope you'll excuse the pre-
sumption) that –

FANNY.

Do you excuse my making you a party concerned, my Lord,   180
and let me interest your heart in my behalf, as my future happiness or misery in a great measure depend –

LORD OGLEBY.

Upon me, Madam?

FANNY.

Upon you, my Lord. [*Sighs.*]

LORD OGLEBY.

There's no standing this: I have caught the infection – her   185
tenderness dissolves me. [*Sighs*].

FANNY.

And should you too severely judge of a rash action which
passion prompted, and modesty has long concealed –

LORD OGLEBY [*Taking her hand*].

Thou amiable creature – command my heart, for it is van-
quished. – Speak but thy virtuous wishes, and enjoy them.   190

FANNY.

I cannot, my Lord – indeed, I cannot. – Mr. Lovewell must
tell you my distresses – and when you know them – pity and
protect me! –

Exit, in tears.

LORD OGLEBY [*Alone*].

How the devil could I bring her to this? It is too much – too
much – I can't bear it – I must give way to this amiable weak-   195
ness – [*Wipes his eyes.*] My heart overflows with sympathy,
and I feel every tenderness I have inspired. – [*Stifles the tear.*]
How blind have I been to the desolation I have made! – How
could I possibly imagine that a little partial attention and tender civilities to this young creature should have gathered to   200
this burst of passion! Can I be a man and withstand it? No –
I'll sacrifice the whole sex to her. – But here comes the father, quite *apropos*. I'll open the matter immediately, settle
business with him, and take the sweet girl down to Ogleby-
house tomorrow morning. – But what the devil! Miss Ster-   205
ling too! What mischief's in the wind now?

Enter Sterling *and* Miss Sterling.

STERLING.

My Lord, your servant! I am attending my daughter here
upon a rather disagreeable affair. Speak to his Lordship,
Betsey!

LORD OGLEBY.

> Your eyes, Miss Sterling – for I always read the eyes of a   210
> young lady – betray some little emotion. – What are your
> commands, Madam?

MISS STERLING.

> I have but too much cause for my emotion, my Lord!

LORD OGLEBY.

> I cannot commend my kinsman's behaviour, Madam. He has
> behaved like a false knight, I must confess. I have heard of his   215
> apostacy. Miss Fanny has informed me of it.

MISS STERLING.

> Miss Fanny's baseness has been the cause of Sir John's incon-
> stancy.

LORD OGLEBY.

> Nay, now, my dear Miss Sterling, your passion transports you
> too far. Sir John may have entertained a passion for Miss   220
> Fanny, but believe me, my dear Miss Sterling, believe me,
> Miss Fanny has no passion for Sir John. [*Conceitedly.*] She has
> a passion, indeed, a most tender passion. She has opened her
> whole soul to me, and I know where her affections are
> placed.   225

MISS STERLING.

> Not upon Mr. Lovewell, my Lord; for I have great reason to
> think that her seeming attachment to him, is, by his consent,
> made use of as a blind to cover her designs upon Sir John.

LORD OGLEBY [*Smiling*].

> Lovewell! No, poor lad! She does not think of him.

MISS STERLING.

> Have a care, my Lord, that both the families are not made the   230
> dupes of Sir John's artifice and my sister's dissimulation! You
> don't know her – indeed, my Lord, you don't know her – a
> base, insinuating, perfidious! – It is too much. – She has been
> beforehand with me, I perceive. Such unnatural behaviour to
> me! – But since I see I can have no redress, I am resolved that   235
> some way or other I will have revenge.

Exit.
Manent Lord Ogleby *and* Sterling.

STERLING.

This is foolish work, my Lord!

LORD OGLEBY.

I have too much sensibility to bear the tears of beauty.

STERLING.

It is touching indeed, my Lord – and very moving for a father.

240

LORD OGLEBY.

To be sure, Sir! – You must be distrest beyond measure! – Wherefore, to divert your too exquisite feelings, suppose we change the subject, and proceed to business.

STERLING.

With all my heart, my Lord!

LORD OGLEBY.

You see, Mr. Sterling, we can make no union in our families by the proposed marriage.

245

STERLING.

And very sorry I am to see it, my Lord.

LORD OGLEBY.

Have you set your heart upon being allied to our house, Mr. Sterling?

STERLING.

'Tis my only wish, at present, my omnium, as I may call it.

250

LORD OGLEBY.

Your wishes shall be fulfilled.

STERLING.

Shall they, my Lord! – but how – how?

LORD OGLEBY.

I'll marry in your family.

STERLING.

What! my sister Heidelberg?

LORD OGLEBY.

You throw me into a cold sweat, Mr. Sterling. No, not your sister – but your daughter.

255

STERLING.

My daughter!

LORD OGLEBY.

Fanny! – now the murder's out!

STERLING.

What *you*, my Lord? –

LORD OGLEBY.

>Yes – I, I, Mr. Sterling!   260

STERLING [*Smiling*].

>No, no, my Lord – that's too much.

LORD OGLEBY.

>Too much? – I don't comprehend you.

STERLING.

>What, you, my Lord, marry my Fanny! – Bless me, what will
>the folks say?

LORD OGLEBY.

>Why, what will they say?   265

STERLING.

>That you're a bold man, my Lord – that's all.

LORD OGLEBY.

>Mr. Sterling, this may be city wit for ought I know. – Do you
>court my alliance?

STERLING.

>To be sure, my Lord.

LORD OGLEBY.

>Then I'll explain. – My nephew won't marry your eldest   270
>daughter – nor I neither. – Your youngest daughter won't
>marry him. – I will marry your youngest daughter –

STERLING.

>What! with a younger daughter's fortune, my Lord?

LORD OGLEBY.

>With any fortune, or no fortune at all, Sir. Love is the idol of
>my heart, and the dæmon Interest sinks before him. So, Sir, as   275
>I said before, I will marry your youngest daughter; your
>youngest daughter will marry me. –

STERLING.

>Who told you so, my Lord?

LORD OGLEBY.

>Her own sweet self, Sir.

STERLING.

>Indeed?   280

LORD OGLEBY.

>Yes, Sir: our affection is mutual; your advantage double and
>treble – your daughter will be a Countess directly – I shall be
>the happiest of beings – and you'll be father to an Earl instead
>of a Baronet.

STERLING.

> But what will my sister say? – and my daughter?   285

LORD OGLEBY.

> I'll manage that matter – nay, if they won't consent, I'll run
> away with your daughter in spite of you.

STERLING.

> Well said, my Lord! – Your spirit's good – I wish you had my
> constitution! – But if you'll venture, I have no objection, if
> my sister has none.   290

LORD OGLEBY.

> I'll answer for your sister, Sir. Apropos! the lawyers are in the
> house – I'll have the articles drawn, and the whole affair con-
> cluded tomorrow morning.

STERLING.

> Very well: and I'll dispatch Lovewell to London immediately
> for some fresh papers I shall want, and I shall leave you to   295
> manage matters with my sister. You must excuse me, my Lord,
> but I can't help laughing at the match – He! he! he! what will
> the folks say?

Exit.

LORD OGLEBY.

> What a fellow am I going to make a father of? – He has no
> more feeling than the post in his warehouse. – But Fanny's   300
> virtues tune me to rapture again, and I won't think of the rest
> of the family.

Enter Lovewell hastily.

LOVEWELL.

> I beg your Lordship's pardon, my Lord; are you alone, my
> Lord?

LORD OGLEBY.

> No, my Lord, I am not alone! I am in the best company.   305

LOVEWELL.

> My Lord!

LORD OGLEBY.

> I never was in such exquisite enchanting company since my
> heart first conceived, or my senses tasted pleasure.

LOVEWELL [*Looking about*].

Where are they, my Lord?

LORD OGLEBY.

In my mind, Sir.   310

LOVEWELL [*Smiling*].

What company have you there, my Lord?

LORD OGLEBY.

My own ideas, Sir, which so croud upon my imagination, and
kindle it to such a delirium of extasy, that wit, wine, musick,
poetry, all combined, and each perfection, are but mere mor-
tal shadows of my felicity.   315

LOVEWELL.

I see that your Lordship is happy, and I rejoice at it.

LORD OGLEBY.

You *shall* rejoice at it, Sir; my felicity shall not selfishly be
confined, but shall spread its influence to the whole circle of
my friends. I need not say, Lovewell, that you shall have your
share of it.   320

LOVEWELL.

Shall I, my Lord? – Then I understand you – you have heard
– Miss Fanny has informed you –

LORD OGLEBY.

She has – I have heard, and she shall be happy – 'tis determined.

LOVEWELL.

Then I have reached the summit of my wishes. – And will   325
your Lordship pardon the folly?

LORD OGLEBY.

O yes, poor creature, how could she help it? – 'Twas unavoid-
able. – Fate and necessity.

LOVEWELL.

It was indeed, my Lord. – Your kindness distracts me.

LORD OGLEBY.

And so it did the poor girl, faith.   330

LOVEWELL.

She trembled to disclose the secret, and declare her affections?

LORD OGLEBY.

The world, I believe, will not think her affections ill placed.

LOVEWELL [*Bowing*].

    – You are too good, my Lord. – And do you really excuse the
rashness of the action?   335

LORD OGLEBY.

    From my very soul, Lovewell.

LOVEWELL.

    Your generosity overpowers me. – [*Bowing*.] – I was afraid of
her meeting with a cold reception.

LORD OGLEBY.

    More fool you then. [*Strikes his breast.*]

        Who pleads her cause with never-failing beauty,   340

        Here finds a full redress.

    She's a fine girl, Lovewell.

LOVEWELL.

    Her beauty, my Lord, is her least merit. She has an under-
standing –

LORD OGLEBY.

    Her choice convinces me of that.   345

LOVEWELL [*Bowing*].

    – That's your Lordship's goodness. Her choice was a disinter-
ested one.

LORD OGLEBY.

    No – no – not altogether – it began with interest, and ended
in passion.

LOVEWELL.

    Indeed, my Lord, if you were acquainted with her goodness   350
of heart, and generosity of mind, as well as you are with the
inferior beauties of her face and person –

LORD OGLEBY.

    I am so perfectly convinced of their excellence, and so totally
of your mind touching every amiable particular of that sweet
girl, that were it not for the cold unfeeling impediments of   355
the law, I would marry her tomorrow morning.

LOVEWELL.

    My Lord!

340-1 Who pleads...redress] Untraced as a quotation; the lines may be Lord
Ogleby's own invention.

LORD OGLEBY.

I would, by all that's honourable in man, and amiable in
woman.

LOVEWELL.

Marry her! – Who do you mean, my Lord?   360

LORD OGLEBY.

Miss Fanny Sterling that is – the Countess of Ogleby that
shall be.

LOVEWELL.

I am astonished.

LORD OGLEBY.

Why, could you expect less from me?

LOVEWELL.

I did not expect this, my Lord.   365

LORD OGLEBY.

Trade and accounts have destroyed your feeling.

LOVEWELL.

No, indeed, my Lord. [*Sighs.*]

LORD OGLEBY.

The moment that love and pity entered my breast, I was resolved to plunge into matrimony, and shorten the girl's tor-
tures – I never do anything by halves; do I, Lovewell?   370

LOVEWELL.

No, indeed, my Lord – [*Sighs.*] – What an accident!

LORD OGLEBY.

What's the matter, Lovewell? Thou seem'st to have lost thy
faculties. Why don't you wish me joy, man?

LOVEWELL.

O, I do, my Lord. [*Sighs.*]

LORD OGLEBY.

She said, that you would explain what she had not power to   375
utter – but I wanted no interpreter for the language of love.

LOVEWELL.

But has your Lordship considered the consequences of your
resolution?

LORD OGLEBY.

No, Sir; I am above consideration, when my desires are kin-
dled.   380

LOVEWELL.

But consider the consequences, my Lord, to your nephew, Sir John.

LORD OGLEBY.

Sir John has considered no consequences himself, Mr. Lovewell.

LOVEWELL.

Mr. Sterling, my Lord, will certainly refuse his daughter to Sir   385
John.

LORD OGLEBY.

Sir John has already refused Mr. Sterling's daughter.

LOVEWELL.

But what will become of Miss Sterling, my Lord?

LORD OGLEBY.

What's that to you? – You may have her, if you will. – I depend upon Mr. Sterling's city-philosophy, to be reconciled to   390
Lord Ogleby's being his son-in-law, instead of Sir John
Melvil, Baronet. Don't you think that your master may be
brought to that, without having recourse to his calculations?
Eh, Lovewell!

LOVEWELL.

But, my Lord, that is not the question.   395

LORD OGLEBY.

Whatever is the question, I'll tell you my answer. – I am in
love with a fine girl, whom I resolve to marry.

Enter Sir John Melvil.

What news have you, Sir John? – You look all hurry and impatience – like a messenger after a battle.

SIR JOHN.

After a battle indeed, my Lord. – I have this day had a severe   400
engagement, and wanting your Lordship as an auxiliary, I
have at last mustered up resolution to declare, what my duty
to you and to myself have demanded from me some time.

LORD OGLEBY.

To the business, then, and be as concise as possible; for I am
upon the wing – eh, Lovewell? [*He smiles, and* Lovewell *bows.*]   405

SIR JOHN.

I find 'tis in vain, my Lord, to struggle against the force of inclination.

LORD OGLEBY.

Very true, Nephew – I am your witness, and will second the motion – shan't I, Lovewell? [*Smiles, and* Lovewell *bows*.]

SIR JOHN.

Your Lordship's generosity encourages me to tell you – that I cannot marry Miss Sterling.   410

LORD OGLEBY.

I am not at all surprized at it – she's a bitter potion, that's the truth of it; but as you were to swallow it, and not I, it was your business, and not mine – any thing more?

SIR JOHN.

But this, my Lord – that I may be permitted to make my addresses to the other sister.   415

LORD OGLEBY.

O yes – by all means – have you any hopes there, Nephew? – Do you think he'll succeed, Lovewell? [*Smiles, and winks at* Lovewell.]

LOVEWELL [*Gravely*].

I think not, my Lord.

LORD OGLEBY.

I think so too, but let the fool try.   420

SIR JOHN.

Will your Lordship favour me with your good offices to remove the chief obstacle to the match, the repugnance of Mrs. Heidelberg?

LORD OGLEBY.

Mrs. Heidelberg! – Had not you better begin with the young lady first? It will save you a great deal of trouble; won't it,   425
Lovewell? – [*Smiles*.] [*Conceitedly*.] – But do what you please, it will be the same thing to me – won't it, Lovewell? – Why don't you laugh at him?

LOVEWELL.

I do, my Lord. [*Forces a smile*.]

SIR JOHN.

And your Lordship will endeavour to prevail on Mrs. Heidel-   430
berg to consent to my marriage with Miss Fanny?

LORD OGLEBY.

    I'll go and speak to Mrs. Heidelberg, about the adorable Fanny, as soon as possible.

SIR JOHN.

    Your generosity transports me.

LORD OGLEBY [*Aside*].

    Poor fellow, what a dupe! He little thinks who's in possession   435
of the town.

SIR JOHN.

    And your Lordship is not offended at this seeming inconstancy.

LORD OGLEBY.

    Not in the least. Miss Fanny's charms will even excuse infidelity. – I look upon women as the *feræ naturæ*, – lawfull   440
game – and every man who is qualified, has a natural right to pursue them; Lovewell as well as you, and I as well as either of you. – Every man shall do his best, without offense to any – what say you, kinsmen?

SIR JOHN.

    You have made me happy, my Lord.   445

LOVEWELL.

    And me, I assure you, my Lord.

LORD OGLEBY.

    And I am superlatively so – *allons donc* – to horse and away, boys! – You to your affairs, and I to mine – suivons l'amour! [*Sings.*]

              Exeunt severally.

---

440 *feræ naturæ*] wild animals

ACT V

SCENE *1, Fanny's apartment.*
Enter Lovewell *and* Fanny – *followed by* Betty.   [V.i]

FANNY.

> Why did you come so soon, Mr. Lovewell? The family is not
> yet in bed, and Betty certainly heard somebody listening near
> the chamber-door.

BETTY.

> My mistress is right, Sir! Evil spirits are abroad; and I am sure
> you are both too good, not to expect mischief from them.   5

LOVEWELL.

> But who can be so curious, or so wicked?

BETTY.

> I think we have wickedness, and curiosity enough in this
> family, Sir, to expect the worst.

FANNY.

> I do expect the worst. – Prithee, Betty, return to the outward
> door, and listen if you hear any body in the gallery; and let us   10
> know directly.

BETTY.

> I warrant you, Madam – the Lord bless you both!

Exit.

FANNY.

> What did my father want with you this evening?

LOVEWELL.

> He gave me the key of his closet, with orders to bring from
> London some papers relating to Lord Ogleby.   15

FANNY.

> And why did you not obey him?

LOVEWELL.

> Because I am certain that his Lordship had opened his heart
> to him about you, and those papers are wanted merely on
> that account – but as we shall discover all tomorrow, there
> will be no occasion for them, and it would be idle in me to   20
> go.

FANNY.

    Hark! – hark! bless me, how I tremble! – I feel the terrors of
guilt – indeed, Mr. Lovewell, this is too much for me.

LOVEWELL.

    And for me too, my sweet Fanny. Your apprehensions make a
cownard of me. But what can alarm you? Your aunt and sister   25
are in their chambers, and you have nothing to fear from the
rest of the family.

FANNY.

    I fear everybody, and everything, and every moment. – My
mind is in continual agitation and dread; – indeed, Mr.
Lovewell, this situation may have very unhappy conse-   30
quences. [*Weeps.*]

LOVEWELL.

    But it shan't. – I would rather tell our story this moment to
all the house, and run the risque of maintaining you by the
hardest labour, than suffer you to remain in this dangerous
perplexity. – What! shall I sacrifice all my best hopes and   35
affections, in your dear health and safety, for the mean, and in
such a case, the meanest consideration – of our fortune! Were
we to be abandoned by all our relations, we have that in our
hearts and minds, will weigh against the most affluent circumstances. – I should not have proposed the secrecy of our   40
marriage, but for your sake; and with hopes that the most
generous sacrifice you have made to love and me, might be
less injurious to you, by waiting a lucky moment of reconciliation.

FANNY.

    Hush! hush! for heaven sake, my dear Lovewell, don't be so   45
warm! – Your generosity gets the better of your prudence;
you will be heard, and we shall be discovered. – I am satisfied,
indeed I am. – Excuse this weakness, this delicacy – this what
you will. – My mind's at peace – indeed it is – think no more
of it, if you love me!   50

LOVEWELL.

    That one word has charmed me, as it always does, to the most
implicit obedience; it would be the worst of ingratitude in
me to distress you a moment. [*Kisses her.*]

        Re-enter Betty.

BETTY [*In a low voice*].

I'm sorry to disturb you.

FANNY.

Ha! What's the matter?   55

LOVEWELL.

Have you heard any body?

BETTY.

Yes, yes, I have, and they have heard *you* too, or I am mistaken
– if they had *seen* you too, we should have been in a fine
quandary.

FANNY.

Prithee don't prate now, Betty!   60

LOVEWELL.

What did you hear?

BETTY.

I was preparing myself, as usual, to take me a little nap.

LOVEWELL.

A nap!

BETTY.

Yes, Sir, a nap; for I watch much better so than wide awake;
and when I had wrapped this handkerchief round my head,   65
for fear of the ear-ach, from the key-hole I thought I heard a
sort of a buzzing, which I first took for a gnat, and shook my
head two or three times, and went so with my hand –

FANNY.

Well – well – and so –

BETTY.

And so, Madam, when I heard Mr. Lovewell a little loud, I   70
heard the buzzing louder too – and pulling off my handkerchief softly – I could hear this sort of noise – [*Makes an indis-
tinct noise like speaking.*]

FANNY.

Well, and what did they say?

BETTY.

Oh! I could not understand a word of what they said.

LOVEWELL.

The outward door is locked?   75

BETTY.

Yes; and I bolted it too, for fear of the worst.

FANNY.

Why did you? They must have heard you, if they were near.

BETTY.

And I did it on purpose, Madam, and coughed a little too, that they might not hear Mr. Lovewell's voice – when I was silent, they were silent, and so I came to tell you.   80

FANNY.

What shall we do?

LOVEWELL.

Fear nothing; we know the worst; it will only bring on our catastrophe a little too soon – but Betty might fancy this noise – she's in the conspiracy, and can make a man of a mouse at any time.   85

BETTY.

I can distinguish a man from a mouse, as well as my betters – I am sorry you think so ill of me, Sir.

FANNY.

He compliments you, don't be a fool! – [*To* Lovewell.] Now you have set her tongue a running, she'll mutter for an hour. I'll go and hearken myself.   90

Exit.

BETTY [*Half aside, and muttering*].

I'll turn my back upon no girl, for sincerity and service.

LOVEWELL.

Thou art first in the world for both; and I will reward you soon, Betty, for one and the other.

BETTY.

I'm not marcenary neither – I can live on a little, with a good *carreter*.   95

Re-enter Fanny.

FANNY.

All seems quiet – suppose, my dear, you go to your own room – I shall be much easier then – and tomorrow we will be prepared for the discovery.

BETTY [*Half aside, and muttering*].

You may discover, if you please; but, for my part, I shall still be secret.   100

LOVEWELL.

Should I leave you now, – if they are still upon the watch, we shall lose the advantage of our delay. – Besides, we should consult upon tomorrow's business. – Let Betty go to her own room, and lock the outward door after her; we can fasten this; and when she thinks all safe, she may return and let me out as   105 usual.

BETTY.

Shall I, Madam?

FANNY.

Do! let me have my way tonight, and you shall command me ever after. – I would not have you surprized here for the world. – Pray leave me! I shall be quite myself again, if you   110 will oblige me.

LOVEWELL.

I live only to oblige you, my sweet Fanny! I'll be gone this moment. [*Going.*]

FANNY.

Let us listen first at the door, that you may not be intercepted. – Betty shall go first, and if they lay hold of her –   115

BETTY.

They'll have the wrong sow by the ear, I can tell them that. [*Going hastily.*]

FANNY.

Softly – softly – Betty! Don't venture out, if you hear a noise. – Softly, I beg of you! – See, Mr. Lovewell, the effects of indiscretion!

LOVEWELL.

But love, Fanny, makes amends for all.   120

Exeunt all softly.

---

116 the wrong...ear] Proverbial since 1546.

SCENE *changes to a gallery,*
which leads to several bed-chambers.

Enter Miss Sterling,
leading Mrs. Heidelberg *in a night-cap.*

MISS STERLING.

This way, dear Madam, and then I'll tell you all.

MRS. HEIDELBERG.

Nay, but Niece – consider a little – don't drag me out in this
figur – let me put on my fly-cap! – If any of my Lord's fammaly, or the counsellors at law, should be stirring, I should be
perdigus disconcarted.   5

MISS STERLING.

But, my dear Madam, a moment is an age, in my situation. I
am sure my sister has been plotting my disgrace and ruin in
that chamber. – O she's all craft and wickedness!

MRS. HEIDELBERG.

Well, but softly, Betsey! – You are all in emotion – your mind
is too much flustrated – you can neither eat nor drink, nor   10
take your natural rest – compose yourself, child; for if we are
not as warysome as they are wicked, we shall disgrace ourselves and the whole fammaly.

MISS STERLING.

We are disgraced already, Madam – Sir John Melvil has for-
saken me; my Lord cares for nobody but himself; or, if for any   15
body, it is my sister; my father, for the sake of a better bargain,
would marry me to a 'Change-broker; so that if you, Madam,
don't continue to be my friend – if you forsake me – if I am
to lose my best hopes and consolation – in your tenderness –
and affec – tions – I had better – at once – give up the matter   20
– and let my sister enjoy – the fruits of her treachery – tram-
ple with scorn upon the rights of her elder sister, the will of
the best of aunts – and the weakness of a too interested father.
[*She pretends to be bursting into tears all this speech.*]

MRS. HEIDELBERG.

Don't Betsey – keep up your spurrit – I hate whimpering – I
am your friend – depend upon me in every partickler – but   25
be composed, and tell me what new mischief you have discovered.

MISS STERLING.

I had no desire to sleep, and would not undress myself, know-
ing that my Machiavel sister would not rest till she had broke
my heart: – I was so uneasy that I could not stay in my room,   30
but when I thought that all the house was quiet, I sent my
maid to discover what was going forward; she immediately
came back and told me that they were in high consultation;
that she had heard only, for it was in the dark, my sister's maid
conduct Sir John Melvil to her mistress, and then lock the   35
door.

MRS. HEIDELBERG.

And how did you conduct yourself in this dalimma?

MISS STERLING.

I returned with her, and could hear a man's voice, though
nothing that they said distinctly; and you may depend upon
it, that Sir John is now in that room, that they have settled the   40
matter, and will run away together before morning, if we
don't prevent them.

MRS. HEIDELBERG.

Why the brazen slut! Has she got her sister's husband (that is
to be) locked up in her chamber! at night too? – I tremble at
the thoughts!   45

MISS STERLING.

Hush, Madam! I hear something.

MRS. HEIDELBERG.

You frighten me – let me put on my fly-cap – I would not be
seen in this figur for the world.

MISS STERLING.

'Tis dark, Madam; you can't be seen.

MRS. HEIDELBERG.

I protest there's a candle coming, and a man too.   50

MISS STERLING.

Nothing but servants; let us retire a moment.

They retire.

Enter Brush *half drunk,*
laying hold of the Chambermaid,
who has a candle in her hand.

CHAMBERMAID.

Be quiet Mr. Brush; I shall drop down with terror!

BRUSH.

But my sweet, and most amiable chambermaid, if you have
no love, you may hearken to a little reason; that cannot possibly do your virtue any harm.   55

CHAMBERMAID.

But you will do me harm, Mr. Brush, and a great deal of
harm, too – pray let me go – I am ruined if they hear you – I
tremble like an asp.

BRUSH.

But they shan't hear us – and if you have a mind to be ruined,
it shall be the making of your fortune, you little slut, you! –   60
Therefore I say it again, if you have no love – hear a little reason!

CHAMBERMAID.

I wonder at your impurence, Mr. Brush, to use me in this
manner; this is not the way to keep me company, I assure you.
– You are a town rake I see, and now you are a little in liquor,   65
you fear nothing.

BRUSH.

Nothing, by heavens, but your frowns, most amiable chamber-maid; I am a little electrified, that's the truth on't; I am
not used to drink Port, and your master's is so heady, that a
pint of it oversets a claret-drinker.   70

CHAMBERMAID.

Don't be rude! Bless me! – I shall be ruined – what will become of me?

BRUSH.

I'll take care of you, by all that's honourable.

CHAMBERMAID.

You are a base man to use me so – I'll cry out, if you don't let
me go – [*Pointing.*] that is Miss Sterling's chamber, that Miss   75
Fanny's, and that Madam Heidelberg's.

---

58 asp] i.e. aspen.

BRUSH.

> And that my Lord Ogleby's, and that my Lady what d'ye call
> 'em: I don't mind much folks when I'm sober, much less
> when I am whimsical – rather above that too.

CHAMBERMAID.

> More shame for you, Mr. Brush! – You terrify me – you have   80
> no modesty.

BRUSH.

> O but I have, my sweet spider-brusher! – For instance, I rev-
> erence Miss Fanny – she's a most delicious morsel and fit for
> a prince – with all my horrors of matrimony, I could marry
> her myself – but for her sister –   85

MISS STERLING.

> There, there, Madam, all in a story!

CHAMBERMAID.

> Bless me, Mr. Brush! – I heard something!

BRUSH.

> Rats, I suppose, that are gnawing the old timbers of the exe-
> crable old dungeon. – If it was mine, I would pull it down,
> and fill your fine canal up with the rubbish; and then I should   90
> get rid of two damned things at once.

CHAMBERMAID.

> Law! law! how you blaspheme! – We shall have the house
> upon our heads for it!

BRUSH.

> No, no, it will last our time – but as I was saying, the eldest
> sister – Miss Jezabel –   95

CHAMBERMAID.

> Is a fine young lady for all your evil tongue.

BRUSH.

> No – we have smoaked her already; and unless she marries
> our old Swiss, she can have none of us – no, no, she won't do
> – we are a little too nice.

CHAMBERMAID.

> You're a monstrous rake, Mr. Brush, and I don't care what   100
> you say.

---

97 smoak] to take note of, or to catch onto.

BRUSH.

> Why, for that matter, my dear, I'm a little inclined to mischief;
> and if you won't have pity upon me, I will break open the
> door and ravish Mrs. Heidelberg.

MRS. HEIDELBERG   [*Coming forward*].

> There's no bearing this – you profligate monster!   105

CHAMBERMAID.

> Ha! I am undone!

BRUSH.

> Zounds! here she is, by all that's monstrous.

Runs off.

MISS STERLING.

> A fine discourse you have had with that fellow!

MRS. HEIDELBERG.

> And fine time of night it is to be here with that drunken
> monster!   110

MISS STERLING.

> What have you, to say for yourself?

CHAMBERMAID.

> I can say nothing. – I am so frightened, and so ashamed – but
> indeed I am vartuous – I am vartuous indeed.

MRS. HEIDELBERG.

> Well, well – don't tremble so; but tell us what you know of
> this horrable plot here.   115

MISS STERLING.

> We'll forgive you, if you'll discover all.

CHAMBERMAID.

> Why, Madam – don't let me betray my fellow-servants – I
> shan't sleep in my bed, if I do.

MRS. HEIDELBERG.

> Then you shall sleep somewhere else tomorrow night.

---

113 vartuous] possibly an echo of Henry Fielding's *Shamela* (1741), in which
Shamela's protestations about her "vartue" are really a cover-up for her sexual
machinations.

CHAMBERMAID.

    O dear! – what shall I do? 120

MRS. HEIDELBERG.

    Tell us this moment, – or I'll turn you out of doors directly.

CHAMBERMAID.

    Why our butler has been treating us below in his pantry. – Mr. Brush forced us to make a kind of a holiday night of it.

MISS STERLING.

    Holiday! for what?

CHAMBERMAID.

    Nay I only made one. 125

MISS STERLING.

    Well, well; but upon what account?

CHAMBERMAID.

    Because, as how, Madam, there was a change in the family they said, – that his honour, Sir John – was to marry Miss Fanny instead of your Ladyship.

MISS STERLING.

    And so you made a holiday for that. – Very fine! 130

CHAMBERMAID.

    I did not make it, Ma'am.

MRS. HEIDELBERG.

    But do you know nothing of Sir John's being to run away with Miss Fanny tonight?

CHAMBERMAID.

    No, indeed, Ma'am.

MISS STERLING.

    Nor of his being now locked up in my sister's chamber? 135

CHAMBERMAID.

    No, as I hope for marcy, Ma'am.

MRS. HEIDELBERG.

    Well, I'll put an end to all this directly – do you run to my brother Sterling –

CHAMBERMAID.

    Now, Ma'am! – 'Tis so very late, Ma'am –

MRS. HEIDELBERG.

    I don't care how late it is. Tell him there are thieves in the 140 house – that the house is o'fire – tell him to come here immediately – go, I say!

CHAMBERMAID.

I will, I will, though I'm frightened out of my wits.

Exit.

MRS. HEIDELBERG.

Do you watch here, my dear; and I'll put myself in order, to
face them. We'll plot 'em, and counter-plot 'em too.   145

Exit into her chamber.

MISS STERLING.

I have as much pleasure in this revenge, as in being made a
countess! – Ha! they are unlocking the door. – Now for it!

Retires.

Fanny's *door is unlocked – and* Betty *comes out with a candle.* Miss
Sterling *approaches her.*

BETTY [*Calling within*].

Sir, Sir! – now's your time – all's clear. [*Seeing* Miss Sterling.]
Stay, stay – not yet – we are watched.

MISS STERLING.

And so you are, Madam Betty! [Miss Sterling *2lays hold of her,*   150
while Betty *locks the door, and puts the key in her pocket.*]

BETTY [*Turning round*].

What's the matter, Madam?

MISS STERLING.

Nay, that you shall tell my father and aunt, Madam.

BETTY.

I am no tell-tale, Madam, and no thief; they'll get nothing
from me.

MISS STERLING.

You have a great deal of courage, Betty; and considering the   155
secrets you have to keep, you have occasion for it.

BETTY.

My mistress shall never repent her good opinion of me,
Ma'am.

Enter Sterling.

STERLING.

What is all this? What's the matter? Why am I disturbed in
this manner?   160
MISS STERLING.

This creature, and my distresses, Sir, will explain the matter.

Re-enter Mrs. Heidelberg, *with another head-dress.*

MRS. HEIDELBERG.

Now I'm prepared for the rancounter – well, brother, have
you heard of this scene of wickedness?
STERLING.

Not I – but what is it? Speak! – I was got into my little closet
– all the lawyers were in bed, and I had almost lost my senses   165
in the confusion of Lord Ogleby's mortgages, when I was
alarmed with a foolish girl, who could hardly speak; and
whether it's fire, or thieves, or murder, or a rape, I am quite in
the dark.
MRS. HEIDELBERG.

No, no, there's no rape, brother! – All parties are willing, I be-   170
lieve.
MISS STERLING.

Who's in that chamber? [*Detaining* Betty, *who seemed to be
stealing away.*]
BETTY.

My mistress.
MISS STERLING.

And who is with your mistress?
BETTY.

Why, who should there be?   175
MISS STERLING.

Open the door then, and let us see!
BETTY.

The door is open, Madam. [Miss Sterling *goes to the door.*] I'd
sooner die than peach!

---

178 peach] Derived from "impeach," i.e. to inform on. Used mainly in the sense
of catching criminals; cf. Mr. Peachum in *The Beggar's Opera.*

Exit hastily.

MISS STERLING.

The door's locked; and she has got the key in her pocket.

MRS. HEIDELBERG.

There's impudence, brother! piping hot from your daughter   180
Fanny's school!

STERLING.

But, zounds! what is all this about? You tell me of a sum total,
and you don't produce the particulars.

MRS. HEIDELBERG.

Sir John Melvil is locked up in your daughter's bed-chamber.
– There is the particular!   185

STERLING.

The devil is he? – That's bad!

MISS STERLING.

And he has been there some time too.

STERLING.

Ditto!

MRS. HEIDELBERG.

Ditto! worse and worse, I say. I'll raise the house, and expose
him to my Lord, and the whole family.   190

STERLING.

By no means! We shall expose ourselves, sister! – The best
way is to insure privately – let me alone! – I'll make him
marry her tomorrow morning.

MISS STERLING.

Make him marry her! This is beyond all patience! – You have
thrown away all your affection; and I shall do as much by my   195
obedience: unnatural fathers make unnatural children. – My
revenge is in my own power, and I'll indulge it. – Had they
made their escape, I should have been exposed to the deri-
sion of the world: – but the deriders shall be derided; and so –
[*Cries out.*] help! help, there! thieves! thieves!   200

MRS. HEIDELBERG.

Tit-for-tat, Betsey! – you are right, my girl.

STERLING.

>Zounds! you'll spoil all – you'll raise the whole family, – the devil's in the girl.

MRS. HEIDELBERG.

>No, no; the devil's in *you*, brother. I am ashamed of your principles. – What! would you connive at your daughter's being 205 locked up with your sister's husband? [*Cries out.*] Help! thieves! thieves! I say!

STERLING.

>Sister, I beg you! – daughter, I command you. – If you have no regard for me, consider yourselves! – We shall lose this opportunity of ennobling our blood, and getting above twenty 210 per cent for our money.

MISS STERLING.

>What, by my disgrace and my sister's triumph! I have a spirit above such mean considerations; and to shew you that it is not a low-bred, vulgar 'Change-Alley spirit – help! help! thieves! thieves! thieves! I say. 215

STERLING.

>Ay, ay, you may save your lungs – the house is in an uproar; – women at best have no discretion; but in a passion they'll fire a house, or burn themselves in it, rather than not be revenged.

>*Enter* Canton, *in a night-gown and slippers.*

CANTON.

>Eh, diable! vat is de raison of dis great noise, this tintamarre? 220

STERLING.

>Ask those ladies, Sir; 'tis of their making.

LORD OGLEBY [*Calls within*].

>Brush! Brush! Canton! where are you? – What's the matter? [*Rings a bell.*] Where are you?

STERLING.

>'Tis my Lord calls, Mr. Canton.

CANTON.

>I come, I come, mi Lor! – 225

>*Exit* Canton. – Lord Ogleby *still rings.*

[V.ii]

FLOWER [*calls within*].

A light! a light here! – Where are the servants? Bring a light for me, and my brothers.

STERLING.

Lights here! Lights for the gentlemen!

Exit Sterling.

MRS. HEIDELBERG.

My brother feels, I see – your sister's turn will come next.

MISS STERLING.

Ay, ay, let it go round, Madam! It is the only comfort I have left. 230

Re-enter Sterling, *with lights, before* Serjeant Flower *(with one boot and a slipper) and* Traverse.

STERLING.

This way, Sir! This way, gentlemen!

FLOWER.

Well, but Mr. Sterling, no danger I hope. – Have they made a burglarious entry? – Are you prepared to repulse them? – I am very much alarmed about thieves at circuit-time. – They 235 would be particularly severe with us gentlemen of the bar.

TRAVERSE.

No danger, Mr. Sterling? – No trespass, I hope?

STERLING.

None, gentlemen, but of those ladies' making.

MRS. HEIDELBERG.

You'll be ashamed to know, gentlemen, that all your labour and studies about this young lady are thrown away – Sir John 240 Melvil is at this moment locked up with this lady's younger sister.

FLOWER.

The thing is a little extraordinary, to be sure – but, why were we to be frightened out of our beds for this? Could not we have try'd this cause tomorrow morning? 245

MISS STERLING.

But, Sir, by tomorrow morning, perhaps, even your assistance
would not have been of any service – the birds now in that
cage would have flown away.

Enter Lord Ogleby *(in his robe de chambre, night cap &c. – leaning on*
Canton.*)*

LORD OGLEBY.

I had rather lose a limb than my night's rest – what's the matter with you all?   250

STERLING.

Ay, ay, 'tis all over! – Here's my Lord too.

LORD OGLEBY.

What is all this shrieking and screaming? – Where's my angelick Fanny. She's safe, I hope!

MRS. HEIDELBERG.

Your angelick Fanny, my Lord, is locked up with your angelick nephew in that chamber.   255

LORD OGLEBY.

My nephew! Then I will be excommunicated.

MRS. HEIDELBERG.

Your nephew, my Lord, has been plotting to run away with
the younger sister; and the younger sister has been plotting to
run away with your nephew: and if we had not watched
them and called up the fammaly, they had been upon the   260
scamper to Scotland by this time.

LORD OGLEBY.

Look'ee, ladies! – I know that Sir John has conceived a violent passion for Miss Fanny; and I know too that Miss Fanny
has conceived a violent passion for another person; and I am
so well convinced of the rectitude of her affections, that I will   265
support them with my fortune, my honour, and my life. – Eh,
shan't I, Mr. Sterling? [*Smiling.*] what say you? –

---

261 Scotland] More particularly Gretna Green, on the Scottish border. It was the
site of many clandestine marriages, since the Marriage Act did not apply in
Scotland.

STERLING [*Sulkily*].

> To be sure, my Lord. – [*Aside.*] These bawling women have been the ruin of every thing.

LORD OGLEBY.

> But come, I'll end this business in a trice – if you, ladies, will   270
> compose yourselves, and Mr. Sterling will insure Miss Fanny from violence, I will engage to draw her from her pillow with a whisper thro' the keyhole.

MRS. HEIDELBERG.

> The horrid creatures! – I say, my Lord, break the door open.

LORD OGLEBY.

> Let me beg of your delicacy not to be too precipitate! – Now   275
> to our experiment! [*Advancing towards the door.*]

MISS STERLING.

> Now, what will they do? – my heart will beat thro' my bosom.

Enter Betty *with the key.*

BETTY.

> There's no occasion for breaking open doors, my Lord; we
> have done nothing that we ought to be ashamed of, and my   280
> mistress shall face her enemies. – [*Going to unlock the door.*]

MRS. HEIDELBERG.

> There's impudence.

LORD OGLEBY.

> The mystery thickens. [*To* Betty.] Lady of the bedchamber!
> open the door, and intreat Sir John Melvil (for these ladies
> will have it that he is there,) to appear and answer to high   285
> crimes and misdemeanors. – Call Sir John Melvil into the court!

Enter Sir John Melvil, *on the other side.*

SIR JOHN.

> I am here, my Lord.

MRS. HEIDELBERG.

> Heyday!

MISS STERLING.

> Astonishment!   290

SIR JOHN.

What is all this alarm and confusion? There is nothing but hurry in the house; what is the reason of it?

LORD OGLEBY.

Because you have been in that chamber; *have* been! nay you *are* there at this moment, as these ladies have protested, so don't deny it –   295

TRAVERSE.

This is the clearest *Alibi* I ever knew, Mr. Serjeant.

FLOWER.

Luce clarius.

LORD OGLEBY.

Upon my word, ladies, if you have often these frolicks, it would be really entertaining to pass a whole summer with you. But come, [*To* Betty] open the door, and intreat your   300
amiable mistress to come forth, and dispel all our doubts with her smiles.

BETTY [*Opening the door. Pertly*].

Madam, you are wanted in this room.

Enter Fanny, *in great confusion.*

MISS STERLING.

You see she's ready dressed – and what confusion she's in!

MRS. HEIDELBERG.

Ready to pack off, bag and baggage! – Her guilt confounds   305
her! –

FLOWER.

Silence in the court, ladies!

FANNY.

I *am* confounded, indeed, Madam!

LORD OGLEBY.

Don't droop, my beauteous lilly! but with your own peculiar modesty declare your state of mind. – [*Smiling.*] Pour convic-   310
tion into their ears, and raptures into mine.

FANNY.

I am at this moment the most unhappy – most distrest – the tumult is too much for my heart – and I want the power to reveal a secret, which to conceal has been the misfortune and misery of my – my – [*Faints away.*]   315

LORD OGLEBY.

    She faints; help, help! for the fairest, and best of women!

BETTY [*Running to her*].

    O my dear mistress! – Help, help, there! –

SIR JOHN.

    Ha! let me fly to her assistance.

[*Speaking all at once*]

        Lovewell *rushes out from the chamber.*

LOVEWELL.

    My Fanny in danger! I can contain no longer. – Prudence were now a crime; all other cares are lost in this! – Speak,   320 speak, to me, my dearest Fanny! – Let me but hear thy voice, open your eyes, and bless me with the smallest sign of life! [*During this speech they are all in amazement.*]

MISS STERLING.

    Lovewell! – I am easy. –

MRS. HEIDELBERG.

    I am thunderstruck!

LORD OGLEBY.

    I am petrify'd!   325

SIR JOHN.

    And I undone!

FANNY [*Recovering*].

    O Lovewell! – even supported by thee, I dare not look my father nor his Lordship in the face.

STERLING.

    What now! Did I not send you to London, Sir?

LORD OGLEBY.

    Eh! – What! – How's this? – By what right and title, have you   330 been half the night in that lady's bed-chamber?

LOVEWELL.

    By that right which makes me the happiest of men; and by a title which I would not forego, for any the best of kings could give me.

BETTY.

    I could cry my eyes out to hear his magnimity.   335

LORD OGLEBY.

    I am annihilated!

STERLING.

> I have been choaked with rage and wonder; but now I can
> speak. – Zounds, what have you to say to me? – Lovewell,
> you are a villain. – You have broke your word with me.

FANNY.

> Indeed, Sir, he has not. – You forbad him to think of me,   340
> when it was out of his power to obey you; we have been
> married these four months.

STERLING.

> And he shan't stay in my house four hours. What baseness and
> treachery! As for you, you shall repent this step as long as you
> live, Madam.   345

FANNY.

> Indeed, Sir, it is impossible to conceive the tortures I have al-
> ready endured in consequence of my disobedience. My heart
> has continually upbraided me for it; and though I was too
> weak to struggle with affection, I feel that I must be miser-
> able for ever without your forgiveness.   350

STERLING.

> Lovewell, you shall leave my house directly; – [To Fanny.] and
> you shall follow him, Madam.

LORD OGLEBY.

> And if they do, I shall receive them into mine. Look ye, Ster-
> ling, there have been some mistakes, which we had all better
> forget for our own sakes; and the best way to forget them is   355
> to forgive the cause of them; which I do from my soul. –
> Poor girl! I swore to support her affection with my life and
> fortune; – 'tis a debt of honour, and must be paid – you swore
> as much too, Mr. Sterling; but your laws in the city will ex-
> cuse *you*, I suppose; for you never strike a ballance without   360
> errors excepted.

STERLING.

> I am a father, my Lord; but for the sake of all other fathers, I
> think I ought not to forgive her, for fear of encouraging
> other silly girls like herself to throw themselves away without
> the consent of their parents.   365

LOVEWELL.

> I hope there will be no danger of that, Sir. Young ladies with
> minds, like my Fanny's, would startle at the very shadow of
> vice; and when they know to what uneasiness only an indis-

cretion has exposed her, her example, instead of encouraging, will rather serve to deter them. 370

MRS. HEIDELBERG.

Indiscretion, quoth a! A mighty pretty delicat word to express disobedience!

LORD OGLEBY.

For my part, I indulge my own passions too much to tyrannize over those of other people. Poor souls, I pity them. And you must forgive them too. Come, come, melt a little of your 375 flint, Mr. Sterling!

STERLING.

Why, why – as to that, my Lord – to be sure he is a relation of yours my Lord – what say *you*, sister Heidelberg?

MRS. HEIDELBERG.

The girl's ruined, and I forgive her.

STERLING.

Well – so do I then. – [*To* Lovewell *and* Fanny, *who seem pre-* 380 *paring to speak.]* Nay, no thanks – there's an end of the matter.

LORD OGLEBY.

But, Lovewell, what makes you dumb all this while?

LOVEWELL.

Your kindness, my Lord – I can scarce believe my own senses – they are all in a tumult of fear, joy, love, expectation, and gratitude; I ever was, and am now more bound in duty to 385 your Lordship; for you, Mr. Sterling, if every moment of my life, spent gratefully in your service, will in some measure compensate the want of fortune, you will perhaps not repent your goodness to me. And you, ladies, I flatter myself, will not for the future suspect me of artifice and intrigue – I shall be 390 happy to oblige, and serve you. – As for you, Sir John –

SIR JOHN.

No apologies to me, Lovewell, I do not deserve any. All I have to offer in excuse for what has happened, is my total ignorance of your situation. Had you dealt a little more openly with me, you would have saved me, and yourself, and that 395 lady (who I hope will pardon my behaviour) a great deal of uneasiness. Give me leave, however, to assure you, that light and capricious as I may have appeared, now my infatuation is over, I have sensibility enough to be ashamed of the part I have acted, and honour enough to rejoice at your happiness. 400

LOVEWELL.

And now, my dearest Fanny, though we are seemingly the happiest of beings, yet all our joys will be dampt, if his Lordship's generosity and Mr. Sterling's forgiveness should not be succeeded by the indulgence, approbation, and consent of these our best benefactors. [*To the audience.*]   405

FINIS.

EPILOGUE

Written by MR. GARRICK.

The Musick by MR. BARTHELEMON.

CHARACTERS OF THE EPILOGUE

Lord Minum	Mr. DODD
Colonel Trill	Mr. VERNON
Sir Patrick Mahony	Mr. MOODY
Miss Crotchet	Mrs. [ABINGTON]
Mrs. Quaver	Mrs. LEE
First Lady	Mrs. BRADSHAW
Second Lady	Miss MILLS
Third Lady	Mrs. DORMAN

SCENE: an Assembly

Several Persons at Cards at different tables;
among the rest Colonel Trill, Lord Minum, Mrs. Quaver,
Sir Patrick Mahony.

At the Quadrille Table.

COLONEL TRILL.
    Ladies, with Leave –
2ND LADY.
              Pass!
3RD LADY.
                  Pass!
MRS. QUAVER.
                       You must do more.
COLONEL TRILL.
    Indeed I can't.   5
MRS. QUAVER.
           I play in Hearts.
COLONEL TRILL.
                   Encore!
2ND LADY.
    What luck!
COLONEL TRILL.
    Tonight at Drury-Lane is play'd
    A Comedy, and *toute nouvelle* – a Spade!   10
    Is not Miss Crotchet at the Play?
MRS. QUAVER.
                    My Niece
    Has made a Party, Sir, to damn the Piece.

At the Whist Table.

LORD MINUM.
    I hate a Play-House – Trump! – It makes me sick.
1ST LADY.
    We're two by Honours, Ma'am.   15
LORD MINUM.
                And we the odd Trick.

Pray do you know the Author, Colonel Trill?
COLONEL TRILL.

I know no Poets, Heaven be prais'd! – Spadille!
1st LADY.

I'll tell you who, my Lord! (*Whispers my Lord.*)
LORD MINUM.

What, he again? 20
"And dwell such daring Souls in little Men?"
Be whose it will, they down our Throats will cram it.
COLONEL TRILL.

O, no. – I have a Club – the best. – We'll damn it.
MRS. QUAVER.

O, Bravo, Colonel! Musick is my Flame.
LORD MINUM.

And mine, by Jupiter! – We've won the Game. 25
COLONEL TRILL.

What, do you all love Musick?
MRS. QUAVER.

No, not Handel's.

And nasty Plays –
LORD MINUM.

Are fit for Goths and Vandals.

Rise from the Table and pay.

From the Piquette Table.

SIR PATRICK.

Well, faith and troth! that Shakespeare was no Fool! 30
COLONEL TRILL.

I'm glad you like him, Sir! – So ends the Pool!

Pay and rise from the Table.

SONG *by the Colonel.*

I hate all their Nonsense,
Their Shakespears and Jonsons,
Their Plays, and their Play-house, and Bards:
'Tis singing, not saying; 35

A Fig for all playing,
But playing, as we do, at Cards!

I love to see Jonas,
Am pleas'd too with Comus;
Each well the Spectator rewards.
So clever, so neat in
Their Tricks, and their Cheating!
Like them we would fain deal our Cards.

SIR PATRICK.

King Lare is touching! – And how fine to see
Ould Hamlet's Ghost! – "To be, or not to be." –   45
What are your Op'ras to Othello's roar?
Oh, he's an Angel of a Blackamoor!

LORD MINUM.

What, when he choaks his Wife? –

COLONEL TRILL.

                                And calls her Whore?

SIR PATRICK.

King Richard calls his Horse – and then Macbeth   50
When e'er he murders – takes away the Breath.
My Blood runs cold at ev'ry Syllable,
To see the Dagger – that's invisible. (*All laugh.*)
Laugh if you please, a pretty Play –

LORD MINUM.

                                   Is pretty.   55

SIR PATRICK.

And when there's Wit in't –

COLONEL TRILL.

                              To be sure 'tis witty.

SIR PATRICK.

I love the Play-house – so light and gay,
With all those Candles, they have ta'en away! (*All laugh.*)
For all your Game, what makes it so much brighter?   60

COLONEL TRILL.

Put out the Light, and then –

LORD MINUM.

                            'Tis so much lighter.

SIR PATRICK.

Pray do you mane, Sirs, more than you express?

COLONEL TRILL.

Just as it happens –

LORD MINUM.

Either more, or less. 65

MRS. QUAVER.

An't you asham'd, Sir? (*to* Sir Patrick.)

SIR PATRICK.

Me! – I seldom blush. –
For little Shakespeare, faith! I'd take a Push!

LORD MINUM.

News, News! – here comes Miss Crotchet from the Play.

Enter Miss Crotchet.

MRS. QUAVER.

Well, Crotchet, what's the News? 70

MISS CROTCHET.

We've lost the Day.

COLONEL TRILL.

Tell us, dear Miss, all you have heard and seen.

MISS CROTCHET.

I'm tired – a Chair – here, take my Capuchin!

LORD MINUM.

And isn't it damn'd, Miss?

MISS CROTCHET.

No, my Lord, not quite: 75
But we shall damn it.

COLONEL TRILL.

When?

MISS CROTCHET.

Tomorrow Night.
There is a Party of us, all of Fashion,
Resolv'd to exterminate this vulgar Passion: 80
A Play-house, what a Place! – I must forswear it.
A little Mischief only makes one bear it.
Such Crowds of City Folks! – so rude and pressing!
And their Horse-Laughs, so hideously distressing.
When e'er we hiss'd, they frown'd and fell a swearing; 85
Like their own Guildhall Giants – fierce and staring!

COLONEL TRILL.

What said the Folks of Fashion? Where they cross?

LORD MINUM.

The rest have no more Judgement than my Horse.

MISS CROTCHET.

Lord Grimly swore 'twas execrable Stuff.

Says one, Why so, my Lord? – My Lord took Snuff.   90

In the first Act Lord George began to doze,

And criticis'd the Author – through his Nose;

So loud indeed, that as his Lordship snor'd,

The Pit turn'd round, and all the Brutes encor'd.

Some Lords, indeed, approv'd the Author's Jokes.   95

LORD MINUM.

We have among us, Miss, *some* foolish Folks.

MISS CROTCHET.

Says poor Lord Simper – Well, now to my Mind

The Piece is good; – but he's both deaf and blind.

SIR PATRICK.

Upon my Soul a very pretty Story!

And Quality appears in all its Glory! –   100

There was some Merit in the Piece, no Doubt;

MISS CROTCHET.

O, to be sure! – if one could find it out.

COLONEL TRILL.

But tell us, Miss, the Subject of the Play.

MISS CROTCHET.

Why, 'twas a Marriage – yes, a Marriage. – Stay!

A Lord, an Aunt, two Sisters, and a Merchant –   105

A Baronet – ten Lawyers – a fat Serjeant –

Are all produc'd – to talk with one another;

And about something make a mighty Pother;

They all go in, and out; and to, and fro;

And talk, and quarrel – as they come and go –   110

Then go to Bed, and then get up – and then –

Scream, faint, scold, kiss, – and go to Bed again.

All laugh.

Such is the Play. – Your Judgment! never sham it.

COLONEL TRILL.
    Oh damn it!
MRS. QUAVER.
           Damn it!   115
1ST LADY.
                   Damn it!
MISS CROTCHET.
                           Damn it!
LORD MINUM.
                                       Damn it!
SIR PATRICK.
    Well, faith, you speak your Minds, and I'll be free –
    Good Night! This Company's too good for me. (*Going.*)   120
COLONEL TRILL.
    Your Judgement, dear Sir Patrick, makes us proud.

                All laugh.

SIR PATRICK.
    Laugh if you please, but pray don't laugh too loud.

                  Exit.

                RECITATIVE.
COLONEL TRILL.
    Now the Barbarian's gone, Miss, tune your Tongue,
    And let us raise our Spirits high with Song!

                RECITATIVE.
MISS CROTCHET.
    Colonel, *de tout mon Cœur* – I've one *in petto,*   125
    Which you shall join, and make it a *Duetto.*

                RECITATIVE.
LORD MINUM.
    Bella Signora, et Amico mio!
    I too will join, and then we'll make a *Trio.* –
COLONEL TRILL.
    Come all and join the full-mouth'd Chorus,
    And drive all Comedy and Tragedy before us!   130

All the Company rise,
and advance to the Front of the Stage.

AIR.

COLONEL TRILL.

Would you ever go to see a Tragedy?

MISS CROTCHET.

Never, never.

COLONEL TRILL.

A Comedy?

LORD MINUM.

Never, never.

Live for ever!   135
Tweedle-dum and Tweedle-dee!

COLONEL TRILL, LORD MINUM and MISS CROTCHET.

Live for ever!
Tweedle-dum and Tweedle-dee!

CHORUS.

Would you ever go to see, &c.

THE

CUNNING-MAN,

A MUSICAL ENTERTAINMENT

IN TWO ACTS

AS IT IS PERFORMED AT THE
THEATRE ROYAL
IN DRURY LANE

Originally written and composed by
M. J.J.ROUSSEAU

Translated and adapted to his original Music
By CHARLES BURNEY.

His business was to pump and wheedle,
And men with their own keys unriddle:
To make to themselves give answer,
For which then pay the Necromancer

HUDIBRAS[1]

The SECOND EDITION

LONDON:
Printed for T. Becket and P.A de Hondt,
Surry-Street, in the Strand
MDCCLXVI

1   HUDIBRAS] Samuel Butler, Hudibras, II.iii. 335-38 (slightly altered)

ADVERTISEMENT

NOTHING but the great reputation of M. Rousseau, and of the following little Drama, would have encouraged the Translator to appear out of his own character before so respectable a tribunal as the Public: but as no production, of the same kind, was ever more admired, or more frequently performed abroad; he was tempted to try its success at home.

The native simplicity and beauty of the original poetry, he could not flatter himself with the hopes of preserving in translation; especially as it was necessary to adjust English words to melodies already made for a foreign language: and, sometimes, to form them into numbers not very common or natural to our own. However, the Airs have been scrupulously preserved from change or mutilation; as the Translator always thought them so pleasing, and so much the music of nature, that the coincidence of the words with the music, would be their greatest recommendation: as they can hardly, indeed, fail to gratify the ear, when sung, however they may displease it, when read.

He hopes, therefore, that the words and the music will always be considered together: with the music he could take but few liberties, not only because it could not be altered without injury, but because it is known to a considerable number of persons, whose ears would be equally disappointed by the omission of sounds to which they were accustomed, or offended by the intrusion of such as were unexpected.

As to the translation, it is submitted to the Public with that consciousness of its defects, which the Translator feels too forcibly not to wish that the difficulties had been less, or that his abilities had been more equal to the task.

Upon rehearsing the Music, it has been thought necessary to retrench the Second Act, for fear of satiety: for though the Airs and Dances, after the reconciliation of Colin *and* Phœbe, *are by no means inferior to the rest in point of composition; yet, as no other business remained to be done after that circumstance but that of mere festivity, the Editor, with some reluctance, submitted to the omission of such Airs, &c. as are printed with inverted commas: which, however, are all published, with the Music, by Mr.* Bremner *in the* Strand.

DRAMATIS PERSONÆ

Cunning–Man	Mr. CHAMPNESS
Colin	Mr. VERNON
Phœbe	Mrs. ARNE
Villagers	

The Translator cannot send this Second Edition to the press, without making his acknowledgements to the Managers of Drury Lane *Theatre, for their great care in getting up this little piece: to the Performers, for their excellent representation of it; and to the Public, for their favourable acceptance of his feeble endeavours to contribute his mite towards their innocent amusements.*

THE CUNNING-MAN

ACT I

The Theatre represents a rural scene with the Cunning-Man*'s House on the Side of a Hill.*

PHŒBE [*Weeping, and wiping her Eyes with her Apron*].

AIR.

Lost is all my peace of mind,
Since my COLIN proves unkind;
    Alas! he's gone for ever.
Ah! since he has learn'd to rove,
Fain would I forget my Love: 5
    Ah me! Ah me! vain is my endeavour.

RECITATIVE.

He lov'd me once – thence flows my pain:
Who then is she has won my swain?
Some charming nymph? – Ah! simple Fair!
And fear'st thou not my ills to share?   10
COLIN for me has ceas'd to burn,
Thou too, ere long, may'st have thy turn –
But why forever thus complain?
Since nought can cure my love,
And all augments my pain!   15

AIR.

"Lost is all my peace of mind,
"Since my COLIN proves unkind:
    "Alas! he's gone for ever.

RECITATIVE.

"I fain would hate him – nay I ought,
"Perhaps he loves me still – vain thought!   20
"Why then for ever from me fly,
"Whose presence once was all my joy?"
Here lives a *CUNNING-MAN*, who well
Our future fortune can foretell.
Ah there he is – of him I'll know
If Love will always prove my foe.

SCENE II   [I.ii]

Cunning-Man *and* Phœbe.

PHŒBE [*Telling money, and hesitating as she approaches the* Cunning-Man, *to whom she gives the money, which she had been counting and folding in a Paper, during the Prelude*].
Will *COLIN* ne'er be mine again?
Tell me, if death must end my pain?
CUNNING-MAN.
I read your heart, and his can tell –
PHŒBE.
O Heav'n! –
CUNNING-MAN.
                    Your grief asswage –   5
PHŒBE.
                                        – Well!

COLIN –
CUNNING-MAN.
                    To you is false of late. –
PHŒBE.
Ah me! I die! – go on –
CUNNING-MAN.
                                        And yet,   10
He always loves you. –
PHŒBE.
                            – What! What said ye? –
CUNNING-MAN.
More artful, but less fair, the lady
Who dwells hard by –

PHŒBE.

— To her he roves?   15

CUNNING-MAN.

But you, I've said, he always loves. —

PHŒBE.

And always flies! —

CUNNING-MAN.

— On one depend,
I soon the Rover back will send.
COLIN is vain, and fond of dress,   20
And that has made him love you less:
An outrage, by my art I swear,
His love hereafter shall repair.

PHŒBE.

AIR.

Had I heard each am'rous ditty
    Breath'd by sparks about the town;   25
Ah! how many spruce and witty
    Lovers there I might have won!

Dress'd as fine as any lady,
    I should then each day have shone,
Bright and beautiful as May-day,   30
    With rich lace and ribbands on.
            Had I heard, &c.
But for love of this Ungrateful,
    I from ev'ry joy could part;
Rich attire to me were hateful,
    If it robb'd him of my heart   35
            Had I heard, &c.

CUNNING-MAN.

RECITATIVE.

His heart I'll soon restore;
Beware you never lose it more;
But first, his passion to increase,
Feign, feign, fair Maid, to love him less.

AIR.

If uneasy, Love increases;   40
If contented, sound he sleeps:

She, who with couqetry teazes,
Fast in chains her shepherd keeps.

PHŒBE.

RECITATIVE.

Resign'd to your advice alone –

CUNNING-MAN.

With COLIN you must change your tone.   45

PHŒBE.

Though hard the task, I yet will feign
To imitate the fickle swain.

AIR.

I'll teaze him and fret him
And seem to forget him,
I'll try ev'ry art to recover my swain: 50
Disguising my sorrow,
The airs I will borrow
Of Flirts and Coquettes, whom at heart I disdain.

CUNNING-MAN.

RECITATIVE.

Be wise, howe'er you fright th'Ingrate,
Nor him too closely imitate. –   55
My Art now says he'll soon be here;
I'll call you when you may appear.

Exit Phœbe.

SCENE III   [I.iii]

CUNNING-MAN.

Tho' COLIN told me all I know
He wonders – I can conjure so –
"And both admire the magick spell,
"By which I find out – what they tell –
Here comes the Swain – and now I'll try   5
To touch his heart with jealousy.

SCENE IV [I.iv]

Cunning-Man *and* Colin.

COLIN.

>By Love, and your instructions, wise,
>I now, for Phœbe, wealth despise. –
>I pleas'd her once, in habit plain,
>What greater bliss can fin'ry gain?

CUNNING-MAN.

>Thou'rt now forgot, so long thou'st rang'd. 5

COLIN.

>Forgot! Oh Heaven! Is Phœbe chang'd?

CUNNING-MAN.

>Did ever woman, young and fair,
>For wrongs like hers, revenge forbear?

COLIN.

AIR.

>No, no, my Phœbe will ne'er deceive me, 10
>　　She will ne'er forget her vows:
>For other Shepherd can she leave me?
>　　Can she be another's spouse?

CUNNING-MAN.

RECITATIVE.

>No Shepherd's now to you preferr'd,
>But 'tis a young, and handsome Lord.

COLIN.

>Who told you so? – 15

CUNNING-MAN.

>　　　　– My art –

COLIN.

>　　　　　　　　– No doubt,
>Your skill all secrets can find out! –
>Alas! how dearly shall I pay
>For being weakly led astray! 20
>Is Phœbe then for ever lost?

CUNNING-MAN.

>By Fortune, Love is often cross'd.
>If pretty fellows we must be,

'Tis sometimes at our cost, you see.

COLIN.

      Oh! lend your aid! –   25

CUNNING-MAN.

                         – Let me consult

My books. – The task is difficult.

Exit Colin.

[*The* Cunning-Man *takes a Conjuring-book out of his pocket, and with his white wand forms a spell during the symphony.*]

          – The charm is ended,

Enter Colin.

Hither comes the maid offended.

COLIN.

      Can I appease her just disdain?   30

      Her pardon may I hope t'obtain?

CUNNING-MAN.

      A heart that's truly kind and tender,

      Propitious soon, a Nymph may render –

      But at yon fountain wait, till she

      Approach, and speak your destiny.   35

Exit Colin.

SCENE V★   [I.v]

CUNNING-MAN.

      But first I'll see th'afflicted Maid,

      And with my sage advice will aid. –

      From Lovers, credulous as these,

      I quickly gain both fame, and fees;

      And shall, when both their union's crown'd,   5

★ As this Piece was thought too long for one Act upon the English Stage, the Translator was obliged to add the words and musick of this Scene, together with the Air, *I'll teaze him and fret him*, &c. in the second Scene, in order to divide it into two Acts. [Burney's note – *ed.*]

Be prais'd by all the neighbours round:
Who hither hasten, from all parts,
To learn who steals their Goods – and Hearts.
For, luckily, they ne'er find out
Whence all our science comes about.   10

AIR.

Some think, in the stars we are able
    Past, present, and future to read:
Some think, from white wand, or gown sable,
    The whole art and mystery proceed.
        But they know not the plan   15
        Of a true Cunning-Man.

When Fortune will rude be or civil,
    Some think we by magic are told;
And some that we deal with the Devil,
    To whom we've our carcasses sold: 20
        But that's not the plan
        Of a true Cunning-Man.

But when folks have been at our dwelling,
    And to us have their secrets betray'd,
We for hearing their tale – and then telling,   25
    Are sure to be very well paid. –
        And this is the plan
        Of a true Cunning-Man.

Exit.
END OF ACT I.

ACT II.

SCENE I

A country prospect.

COLIN [*Solo*].

AIR.

I soon my charming Nymph shall view;
Fine houses, grandeur, wealth, adieu!
   No more by you my love is crost.
     If my tears,
      My anxious cares,   5
Can touch the maid whom I adore,
I then may see renew'd once more
   Those happy moments I have lost!
I then may see, &c.

Love with love, if but repaid,
   Is there need of other bliss?   10
Give me back thy heart, sweet Maid!
   Colin has restor'd thee his.

Now my crook, and oaten reed,
   Shall my only trappings prove:
Bless'd with Phœbe, shall I need   15
   Other treasures than her love?
Love with love, &c.

What great Lords did ev'ry hour
   For my Phœbe fondly sigh!
Yet, in spight of all their pow'r,   20
   They less happy are than I.

Love with love, if but repaid,
   Is there need of other bliss?
Give me back thy heart, sweet Maid!
   Colin has restor'd thee his.   25

SCENE II

Colin *and* Phœbe

COLIN [*Aside*].

RECITATIVE. ACCOMPANIED.

Ah! here she comes, I tremble at her sight. –
I'll e'en retreat – she's lost if once I fly.

PHŒBE [*Aside*].

He sees me now – I'm in a dreadful fright! –
Be still, my heart. –

COLIN [*Aside*].

                – I'll e'en my fortune try.   5

PHŒBE [*Aside*].

I'm nearer got than I at first design'd.

COLIN [*Aside*].

On, on I'll go; there's no retreat, I find –

[*To* Phœbe, *in a soothing and confused tone of voice.*]

Sweet Phœbe! are you angry, say?
I Colin am – O look this way!

PHŒBE.

Me Colin lov'd – Colin was true –   10
I see not Colin – yet see you.

COLIN.

My heart has never chang'd – some vile
Enchantment did my sense beguile.
But our sagacious, Cunning-Man,
Had broke the charm – and now, again,   15
In spite of envy, you will find,
I'm Colin still, and still more kind.

PHŒBE.

I, in my turn, am now pursu'd
By spell, which ne'er can be subdu'd
By Cunning-Man –   20

COLIN.

                – Unhappy me!

PHŒBE.
>A youth of greater constancy –

COLIN.
>Ah! death will quickly end my smart,
>If Phœbe from her vows depart!

PHŒBE.
>Your future cares in vain will prove,   25
>No, Colin, you no more I love.

COLIN.

AIR.

>Your love from me's not yet departed
>>No, consult first well your breast;
>To kill me, were you so hard-hearted,
>>Would destroy your peace and rest.   30

PHŒBE.
>[*Aside.*] Ah me! – [*To* Colin.] No, by you betray'd.
>Useless all your cares will prove
>Since Colin now I cease to love.

COLIN.
>I'm then undone! – Ah! cruel Maid!
>Since 'tis your will that I should die,   35
>For ever I'll the village fly.

Going.

PHŒBE.
>Ah, Colin! –

COLIN [*Returning*].
>>– What?

PHŒBE.
>>– And wilt thou go?

COLIN.
>Must I then feel the double woe,   40
>To lose my heart, forego thy charms,
>And see thee in a rival's arms?

PHŒBE.

DUET.

>While I my Colin knew to please,
>>No other wish I had to name:

COLIN.

> I thought my joy could never cease,
>> While Phœbe own'd a mutual flame. 45

PHŒBE.

> But since to me his heart's denied,
>> Mine's given to another swain.

COLIN.

> Ah! since the gentle knot's untied,
>> Does another bliss remain? – 50
> My dear Phœbe then will leave me!

PHŒBE.

> I fear a lover who'll deceive me.

BOTH.

> I disengage me in my turn:
>> My heart's now in a peaceful state,
>> And will, if possible, forget 55
>
> That e'er it did for $\begin{cases} \text{Colin} \\ \text{Phœbe} \end{cases}$ burn.

COLIN.

> However great the wealth or pleasure
>> Which new engagements would have given:
> Phœbe, I thought, a greater treasure
>> Than all the goods that's under Heaven. 60

PHŒBE.

> Though a young and charming Lord
>> Has often woo'd me to his arms;
> *COLIN* was fondly then preferr'd
>> To all his proffer'd wealth and charms.

COLIN.

> Ah! my Phœbe! 65

PHŒBE.

> Ah! too fickle Swain!
> Must I then love, in spight of all disdain?

PRELUDE.

[Phœbe *reminds* Colin *of a ribband in his hat,
which had been given him by the lady:
He throws it away, and she gives him a more ordinary one,
which he receives with transport.*]

DUET.

COLIN.

    Colin now his faith has plighted,
      Nor longer will rove.

PHŒBE.

    Phœbe now her heart has plighted,   70
      And constant will prove.

BOTH.

    When by Hymen united,
      How endless our love!

SCENE III   [II.iii]

Cunning-Man, Colin, Phœbe.

CUNNING-MAN.

    My pow'r has caus'd th'enchantment dire to cease,
    And, spight of envy, giv'n your love encrease.

[*They severally offer him a present.*]

COLIN.

    Our thanks by this are ill express'd.
CUNNING-MAN [*Receiving with both hands*].
    I'm amply paid, if you are bless'd.

AIR.

    Haste, haste ye maidens fair,   5
    Haste, haste ye jocund swains,
      Assemble here, assemble here,
    And imitate this pair.
    Gay shepherds quit the Plains,
    Fair nymphs from village haste,   10

Their joy, in tuneful strains,
Come sing, and learn to taste.

SCENE IV   [II.iv]

Colin, Phœbe, Cunning-Man
with a company of Villagers, *of both sexes.*

DANCE.

CHORUS [*With the* Cunning-Man].
    Since Colin now has ceas'd to range,
    Let's celebrate the happy change:
    May their home be blest with peace,
    And their love each day encrease!
CHORUS [*Without the* Cunning-Man].
    "Sing ye nymphs and shepherds the praises,   5
        "Loudly sing of our Cunning-Man:
    "A dead passion to life he raises,
        "And makes true and happy the swain."

PASTORAL DANCE.

[*The Shepherdesses give a Nosegay to* Colin, *who immediately presents
it to* Phœbe.]

[*The Shepherds give* Phœbe *a Nosegay, who in her Turn,
gives it to* Colin.]

AIR.

COLIN.
    "In my cottage obscure,
        "New evils for ever I share;   10
    "Now cold, now heat I endure,
        "Nor am e'er free from labour and care.

    "But, if Phœbe's my bride,
        "And will all my past follies forget,
    "While with her I reside,   15

"A thatch'd house will have nought to regret.

"From the mead or the field,
    "If fatigu'd, I return, when 'tis night,
"New life, new vigour she'll yield,
    "New comfort and joy to my sight.   20

"Ere the sun gilds the plains,
    "Or reddens the tops of the groves,
"I shall charm all my pains
    "By singing with rapture our loves.

CUNNING-MAN.

"We all with zeal must here essay   25
"To signalize ourselves today:
"And since I cannot jump so high as you,
"My part shall be to sing a song that's new.

[*Pulls a song out of his pocket and sings.*]

AIR.

"Sometimes a passion's rais'd by art,   30
"Sometimes 'tis nature gives the smart;
"Though courtly Lovers well can charm,
"Yet village hearts are still more warm.
"Love is just like April weather,
"Ne'er the same an hour together:
"Froward, fickle, wanton, wild   35
"Nothing, nothing but a child.

COLIN.

" 'Tis but a child, 'tis but a child.

RECITATIVE.

[*To the* Cunning-Man, *who is putting the song in his pocket.*]

"Stay, stay, there other verses are —
"And very pretty too, I swear.

PHŒBE.

"Let's see, let's see — I eager burn,   40
"To sing a Stanza in my turn."

AIR.

Though here, alone with nature Love
In simple guise delights to rove;
In other places, he no less
Affects the borrow'd charm of dress.   45

Love is just like April weather,
Ne'er the same an hour together:
Froward, fickle, wanton, wild
Nothing, nothing but a child.

CHORUS.

'Tis but a child, 'tis but a child.   50

COLIN.

A cherish'd flame we often see
Produc'd by ingenuity;
A fickle heart we oft retain
By arts coquettish, light and vain,
    Love is just like April, &c.

PHŒBE.

"Yet Love disposes of us all,   55
"At his own fancy's fickle call:
"Black jealousy he now permits
"Now punishes our jealous fits.
    "Love is just like April, &c.

COLIN.

"From Fair to Fair, while sickly tost,   60
"The happy moment's often lost:
"A Swain quite constant oft will find,
"He's less belov'd, than one unkind.
    "Love is just like April, &c.

PHŒBE.

"On Mortals each caprice to prove,
"Now smiles, now tears awaken love:
"Rebuff'd – Rebuff'd – [*Finds it difficult to read.*]   65
COLIN [*Who helps her to decypher it*].
    "Rebuff'd by rigour, far he flies,

PHŒBE.

    "By favours weaken'd, faints, and dies.

BOTH.

    "Love is just like April weather,

"Ne'er the same an hour together,
"Froward, fickle, wanton, wild,   70
"Nothing, nothing but a child.

CHORUS.

" 'Tis a child, 'tis a child.

AIR.

PHŒBE.

"United with the Swain I love,
"My life a round of joy will prove;
"Of grief we ne'er can feel the sting,   75
"While thus we laugh and dance and sing.
          "What a blessing is life!
          "If 'tis season'd by love!
          "No care, no sorrow, or strife,
          "Can its joy e'er remove.   80
          "Thus a gentle river flows,
          "Meand'ring as it goes,
"Through flow'ry meads which grace its way
"With all that's fair, and sweet, and gay

"United with the Swain I love,   85
"My life a round of joy will prove;
"Of grief we ne'er can feel the sting,
"While thus we laugh, and dance, and sing."

AIR.

Let us now dance with mirth and glee,   90
          Lasses and lads, beat, beat the ground;
Let us now dance, all under this tree,
          To the sweet pipe's enliv'ning sound.
CHORUS [*Repeats with her. The Villagers dancing at the same time*].
          Let us now dance, &c.

Let us first sing, then dance to each Air,
          And in the joy that all may have a part,
Let each Swain dance with his fav'rite Fair,   95
          And let each Lass have the Lad of her heart.
          Then let us now dance, &c.

Though noise and splendour they boast of in town,
More heart-felt enjoyments our festivals crown:
       While dance and song,   100
       Our bliss prolong,
       And beauty warms,
       With artless charms –
What musick e'er with our pipes can compare?

Then let us all dance with mirth and glee   105
Lasses and Lads, beat, beat the ground;
Let us then dance all under this tree
To the sweet pipe's enliv'ning sound.

FINIS.

THE

REHEARSAL:

OR,

BAYS in PETTICOATS.

A

COMEDY

In Two ACTS.

As it is performed at the

Theatre Royal in *Drury-Lane*.

Written by Mrs. CLIVE.

The Music compofed by Dr. BOYCE.

LONDON:
Printed for R. Dodsley in Pall-mall. 1753.
Price One Shilling.

ADVERTISEMENT

This little Piece was written above three Years since, and acted for my Bene-
fit.—The last Scene was an Addition the Year after. Whatever Faults are in
it, I hope, will be pardoned, when I inform the Public, I had at first no De-
sign of printing it; and do it now at the Request of my Friends, who (as it
met with so much Indulgence from the Audience) thought it might give 5
some Pleasure in the reading.—The Songs were written by a Gentleman.

I take this Opportunity to assure the Public, I am, with great Gratitude
and Respect,

Their most Obliged,
Humble Servant.   10
C. Clive.

---

7 William Boyce (1711-1779), who, along with Thomas Arne, was composer at
   Drury-Lane Theatre.

PERSONS

MEN.

Witling	Mr. WOODWARD.
Sir Albany Odelove	Mr. SHUTER.
Tom	Mr. MOZEEN.
Prompter	Mr. CROSS.

WOMEN.

Mrs. Hazard	Mrs. CLIVE.
Miss Giggle	Miss MINORS.
Miss Crotchet	Miss HIPPISLEY.
Miss Sidle	Mrs. SIMSON.
Miss Dawdle	Mrs. TOOGOOD.
Gatty	Mrs. BENNETT.
[Miss.]	

PASTORAL CHARACTERS.

Corydon	Mr. BEARD.
Miranda	Miss THOMAS.
Marcella	Mrs. CLIVE.

THE REHEARSAL

OR, BAYES IN PETTYCOATES

ACT I

SCENE 1

A Dressing-Room in Mrs. Hazard's House.
(Gatty preparing the Toylet.)
Enter Tom with Tea Things.

GATTY.

Well, I believe we are at present the most melancholy Family
in Town, that used to be the merriest. Since these Devils, the
Muses (as my Lady calls 'em) have got into the House, they
have turned her Head, and she distracts every body about
her. She really was once a sweet-tempered Woman; but now   5
I can't speak, or stir, but she flies at me, and says I have flur-
ried her out of one of the finest Thoughts! − Hang her! I
wish her Farce may be hissed off the Stage.

TOM.

That's but a foolish kind of Wish; for if she's so sweet-tempered now, what do you think she'll be then?   10

GATTY.

I don't care what she'll be; for I'm determined not to stay
with her. I am sure she uses me like her Dog.

TOM.

Does she? − Then you are an ungrateful Hussey to complain:
for she is fonder of that, than ever she was of her Husband. −
I fancy this Farce of her's is horrid Stuff: for I observe, all her   15
Visitors she reads it to (which is indeed every body that
comes to the House) whisper as they come down Stairs, and
laugh ready to kill themselves.

GATTY.

Yes, but that's at her Assurance. Why, do you know 'tis none of her own? A Gentleman only lent it to her to read; he has been ill a great while at *Bath*; so she has taken the Advantage of that, made some little Alterations, had it set to Music, and has introduced it to the Stage as a Performance of her own.

TOM.

I hear Mr. *Surly*, that every body thought she was going to be married to, is so enraged at her, that he'll never speak to her, or see her again. One of his Footmen told me of it yesterday, as a great Secret, so I promised him never to mention it. – Don't you hear her Bell ring? [*Rings.*]

GATTY.

Hear her! yes, yes, I hear her; but I should have a fine Time on't, if I was to go to her, as often as she takes it in her Head to ring. [*Rings again.*] Ay, ay, ring away.

TOM.

Ay, ay, ring away – I'gad here she comes. I wish you well off.

Exit.
Enter Mrs. Hazard.

MRS. HAZARD.

Why, what is the Meaning I must ring for an Hour, and none of ye will come near me, ye Animals? –

GATTY.

I was coming as fast as I could.

MRS. HAZARD.

As fast as you could! Why, you move like a Snail that has been trod upon, you creeping Creature. – Let me die, but she has provoked me into a fine Simile. Come, get the Things to dress me instantaneously. [*Tom with Tea and Coffee. She repeats Recitative,* Oh Corydon, &c.] You, *Tom,* I'm at home to no human Being this Morning but Mr. *Witling.* I've promised to carry him to the *Rehearsal* with me. [*Repeats Recitative,* Gatty *waiting with her Cap.*]

GATTY.

Madam, will you please have your Cap on?

MRS. HAZARD.

No! you Ideot; how durst you interrupt me, when you saw
me so engaged? As I am a Critic, this Creature will distract
me! – Give me my Bottle of Salts. – She has ruined one of
the finest Conclusions. – O *Cor.* – Lord! I can't sing a Note.
– What are you doing? 50

GATTY.

Lord, Madam, I can't find them!

MRS. HAZARD.

Here's a provoking Devil! sees 'em in my Hand, and would
not tell me of it! Get out of my Sight. [*Repeats Recitative.*]
Why, where are you going? Am I to dress myself?

GATTY.

Madam, Mr. *Witling.* 55

Enter Witling.

WITLING.

My dear Widow! you're hard at it I see. Come, give me
some Tea. What is it, your Prologue, or Epilogue, pray?

MRS. HAZARD.

O Lord! dear *Witling!* – Don't be ridiculous; for I'm in a horrid Humour.

WITLING.

Yes; and a horrid Dress too, I think. Why, 'tis almost ten. – 60
What is this, your Rehearsal Habiliment?

MRS. HAZARD.

Why, that Creature that you see standing there, won't give
me any thing to put on.

WITLING.

Well, do you know I have had such a Quarrel with *Frank
Surly* upon your Account? We met last Night at Lady *Betty* 65
Brag's Rout; – there was a vast deal of Company, – and they
were all talking of your new Piece.

MRS. HAZARD.

So, I suppose I was finely worried.

---

66 Rout] A large fashionable assembly, usually attended by great crowds.

WITLING.

> You shall hear: as soon as ever it was mentioned, we all burst
> out a laughing.

MRS. HAZARD.

> You did! – and pray what did you laugh at?

WITLING.

> Hey! – why – oh, at *Frank Surly*; he looked so like a – ha, ha,
> ha, i'gad I can't find a Simile that can give you an Idea of
> such a Face. Oh, thinks I, my dear, you're in a fine Humour
> to make us some Diversion. So, says I, *Frank*, I hear the   75
> Match is quite concluded between Mrs. *Hazard* and you; and
> that she has fixed the first Night of her Comedy for your
> Wedding-Night. – Sir, says he (with a very grave Face) you
> may say what you please of Mrs. *Hazard*; for as she's going to
> expose herself, she must expect that every Fool will be as im-   80
> pertinent as she is ridiculous: – but I would advise you not to
> mention my Name any more in that Manner, for, if you do,
> I shall take it extremely ill. Lord! says Miss *Giggle*, Mr. *Surly*,
> how can you be so cross? Expose herself! – I'll swear, I be-
> lieve Mrs. *Hazard* can write a very pretty Play, for she has a   85
> great deal of Wit and Humour. – Wit and Humour! says he,
> where there is not ten Women in the Creation that have
> Sense enough to write a consistent *N.B.* – Marry her! I
> would sooner marry a Woman that had been detected in ten
> Amours, than one, who, in Defiance to all Advice, and with-   90
> out the Pretence that most People write for, (for every body
> knows she's a Woman of Fortune) will convince the whole
> World she's an Ideot.

MRS. HAZARD.

> A Bear! a Brute! Let me hear no more of him.

WITLING.

> Yes, but I must tell you a very good thing that I said to him.   95

MRS. HAZARD.

> No, that you can't I'm sure, *Witling*; for you never said a
> good thing in your Life.

WITLING.

> Nay, why should you be so ill-natured to me? I'm sure I
> took your Part. Why, says I, *Frank*, how can you be such a
> Fool to quarrel with her? I wish she liked me half so well, as 100
> I'm sure she does you; she should write, and be hanged if she

would for any thing I cared; for let them do what they will
with her Performance, they can't damn her eight hundred a
Year.

MRS. HAZARD.

You said so, did you? 105

WITLING.

I said so! – No; Lord, Child! – How could you think I could
say such a thing. No, no, to be sure it was said by somebody
in the Company. But upon Honour I don't know who.

MRS. HAZARD [Aside].

What a Wretch is this? – But he is to carry a Party for me for
the first Night; so I must not quarrel with him. 110

WITLING.

Well, but my dear Hazard, when does your Farce come out?

MRS. HAZARD.

Why some time next Week; this is to be last Rehearsal: and
the Managers have promised they shall all be dressed, that we
may see exactly what Effect it will have.

WITLING.

Well, but don't your Heart ache, when you think of the first 115
Night? hey. –

MRS. HAZARD.

Not in the least; the Town never hiss any thing that is introduced to them, by a Person of Consequence and Breeding.
Because they are sure they'll have nothing low.

WITLING.

Ay, but they mayn't be so sure they'll have nothing foolish. 120

MRS. HAZARD.

Ha! – Why perhaps they mayn't find out one so soon as
t'other. Ha, ha, ha, well, let me die if that is not a very good
thing. – But 'tis well for me, Witling, the Town don't hear
me; not that I mean quite what I say neither, for to do them
Justice, they're generally in the right in their Censure; tho' 125
sometimes indeed they will out of Humanity forgive an
Author Stupidity, and overlook his being a Fool; provided
he will do them the Favour not to be a Beast; for which
Reason, Witling, I have taken great care to be delicate; I may
be dull, but I'm delicate; so that I'm not at all afraid of the 130
Town: I wish I could say as much of the Performers: Lord,
what pity 'tis the great Tragedy Actors can't sing! I'm about a

new Thing, which I shall call a Burletto, which I take from some Incidents in *Don Quixote*, that I believe will be as high Humour, as was ever brought upon the Stage. But then I 135 shall want Actors; oh! if that dear *Garrick* could but sing, what a *Don Quixote* he'd make!

WITLING.

Don't you think *Barry* would be a better! He's so tall you know, and so finely made for't. If I was to advise, I would carry that to *Covent-Garden*. 140

MRS. HAZARD.

Covent-Garden! Lord, I wouldn't think of it, it stands in such a bad Air.

WITLING.

Bad Air!

MRS. HAZARD.

Ay; the Actors can't play there above three Days a Week. They have more need of a Physician, than a Poet, at that 145 House.

WITLING.

But pray Madam, you say you are to call your new Thing, a Burletto; what is a Burletto?

MRS. HAZARD.

What is a Burletto? What haven't you seen one at the *Hay-market?* 150

WITLING.

Yes; but I don't know what it is for all that.

MRS HAZARD.

Don't you! Why then, let me die if I can tell you, but I believe it's a kind of poor Relation to an Opera.

---

133 Burletto] More properly, Burletta.

134 *Don Quixote*] Cervantes' 1616 novel was well-known to English readers in the eighteenth century. The novelist Smollett prepared a translation of both parts, and based *Sir Lancelot Greaves* (1760-1761) on it. The premise was also adapted – and to some degree lampooned – by Charlotte Lennox in *The Female Quixote* (1753).

138 *Barry*] Spranger Barry (1717?-1777), long rival of Garrick, first at Drury Lane, then at Covent Garden.

149] *Hay-market*] The Haymarket Opera House – also known as the Queen's Theatre, the King's Theatre, and Her Majesty's Opera House – featured Italian opera and musical theatre. The Opera House burned down in 1789.

WITLING.

Pray how many Characters have you in this thing?

MRS. HAZARD.

Why I have but three; for as I was observing, there's so few 155
of them that can sing: nay I have but two indeed that are rational, for I have made one of them mad.

WITLING.

And who is to act that, pray?

MRS. HAZARD.

Why Mrs. *Clive* to be sure; tho' I wish she don't spoil it; for
she's so conceited, and insolent, that she won't let me teach 160
it her. You must know when I told her I had a Part for her in
a Performance of mine, in the prettiest manner I was able,
(for one must be civil to these sort of People when one wants
them) says she, Indeed, Madam, I must see the whole Piece,
for I shall take no Part in a new thing, without chusing that 165
which I think I can act best. I have been a great Sufferer already, by the Manager's not doing justice to my Genius; but
I hope I shall next Year convince the Town, what fine Judgment they have: for I intend to play a capital Tragedy Part
for my own Benefit. 170

WITLING.

And what did you say to her, pray?

MRS. HAZARD.

Say to her! Why do you think I would venture to expostu-
late with her? – No, I desired Mr. *Garrick* would take her in
hand; so he ordered her the Part of the Mad-woman directly. 175

WITLING.

Well, I think the Town will be vastly obliged to you, for
giving them such an Entertainment, as I am told it is from
every body that has heard it; tho' the ill-natured part of your
Acquaintance say 'tis none of your own.

MRS. HAZARD.

Why whose do they say it is, pray? – Not yours, *Witling*; not 180
quite so bad as that I hope. No, my Motive for writing, was
really Compassion; the Town has been so overwhelmed
with Tragedies lately, that they are in one entire Fit of the
Vapours. – They think they love 'em, but it's no such thing.
I was there one Night this Season at a Tragedy, and there 185

was such an universal Yawn in the House, that if it had not
been for a great Quantity of Drums and Trumpets, that most
judiciously every now and then came in their Relief, the
whole Audience would have fallen asleep.

Enter Tom.

TOM.

Madam, there's a young Miss desires to speak to you upon   190
particular Business.

WITLING.

Heark'e, *Tom*, are you sure 'tis a young Miss? – If 'tis an old
one, don't let her come up; for they are a Sort of Creatures I
have a great Aversion to.

MRS. HAZARD.

Why, thou impertinent, stupid Wretch! Did not I bid you to   195
deny me to every body? don't you know I am going out this
Instant?

TOM.

Madam, 'tis not my fault; I was not below, and they let her
in.

MRS. HAZARD.

I don't believe there is a Woman in the World has such a   200
Collection of Devils in her House as I have.

Enter Miss.

MISS.

Mame, – your Servant. – Not to interrupt you.

MRS. HAZARD.

Yes, Miss; but you have done that. – What is your Business
pray?

MISS.

Why, Mame – I was informed as how that there was a new   205
Play of yours, Mame, a-coming out upon the Stage, with
some Singing in't.

SD Miss] Not listed in the Dramatis Personae.

MRS. HAZARD.

> Coming out upon the Stage! (Lord! where could this Crea-
> ture come from!) Well, Miss.

MISS.

> So, Mame, I have a Desire, (not that I have any Occasion),   210
> but 'tis my Fancy, Mame, to come and sing upon the Stage.

MRS. HAZARD.

> And a very odd Fancy I believe it is. – Well, Miss, you say, it
> is your Fancy to sing upon the Stage; but, pray are you quali-
> fied?

MISS.

> O yes, Mame; I have very good Friends.   215

MRS. HAZARD.

> The Girl's a Natural! – Why, Miss, that's a very great Happi-
> ness; but I believe a good Voice would be more material to
> your Fancy; – I suppose you have a good Voice.

MISS.

> No, Mame; I can't say I have much Voice.

MRS. HAZARD.

> Ha, ha, she's delightful! I am glad they let her in. Well, Miss,   220
> to be sure then you are a Mistress!

MISS.

> Mame – What do you mean?

MRS. HAZARD.

> Ha, ha; I say, I imagine you understand Music perfectly well.

MISS.

> No, Mame, I never learnt in my Life; but 'tis my Fancy.

WITLING [*Aside*].

> Miss is a very pretty Girl, I wish she'd take a Fancy to me; I   225
> believe it would answer my purpose better than singing will
> hers.

MRS. HAZARD.

> Well; but, my Dear, as you confess you have neither Voice
> nor Judgment, to be sure you have a particular fine Ear!

MISS.

> Yes, Mame, I've a very good Ear – that is, when I sing by   230
> myself; but the Music always puts me out.

---

216 Natural] Simpleton.

MRS. HAZARD.

Ha, ha. Well, Child, you have given an exceeding good Account of yourself, and I believe will make a very extraordinary Performer.

MISS.

Thank you, Mame. Yes, I believe I shall do very well in 235
time.

WITLING.

Pray, Miss, won't you favour us with a Song?

MISS.

Yes, Sir; if you please, I'll sing *Powerful Guardians of all Nature*: I've brought it with me.

MRS. HAZARD.

Pray let's hear it. [Miss *sings.*] Oh fie! Miss! that will never 240
do; you speak your Words as plain as a Parish-Girl; the Audience will never endure you in this kind of Singing, if they understand what you say: you must give your Words the *Italian* Accent, Child. – Come, you shall hear me. [Mrs. Hazard *sings in the* Italian *manner.*] There, Miss, that's the Taste of 245
singing now. – But I must beg you would excuse me at present; I'm going to the Play-house, and will certainly speak to the Managers about you; for I dare believe you'll make a prodigious Figure upon the Stage.

WITLING.

That you will indeed, Miss. – [*Aside.*] The strangest that ever 250
was seen there.

MISS.

Sir, I thank you. Mame, I thank you. Mame, I'll wait on you another Time.

MRS. HAZARD.

Miss, your Servant.

Exit Miss.

– No; that you shall not do, I promise you. 255

Enter Tom.

TOM.

> Madam, your Chair has been waiting a great while; 'tis after
> Ten, above half an Hour.

MRS. HAZARD.

> My Stars! this driveling Girl has ruined me. Here, *Gatty*, get
> me my Shade; I'll go as I am.

WITLING.

> Shan't I set you down?   260

MRS. HAZARD.

> Oh! not for the World! An Authoress to be seen in the Char-
> iot of a Fool, would be the greatest Absurdity in Nature; we
> shall meet at the House.

WITLING.

> Very well, Mame, and I shall be in the Pit the first Night; re-
> member that. – Come, give me your Hand, however.   265

Exeunt.

ACT II

SCENE, The Play-house.

Enter Mrs. Hazard, Mr. Witling, and Mr. Cross.

MRS. HAZARD.

Mr. *Cross*, your Servant. Has any body been to ask for me this Morning?

MR. CROSS.

Not any body, Madam.

MRS. HAZARD.

Well, that's very surprizing! I expected Half the Town would have been trying to get in: but 'tis better as 'tis; for   5 they would have only interrupted the *Rehearsal*. So, Mr. *Cross*, I'll be denied to every body. Well, *Witling*, how do you like the Play-house in a Morning?

WITLING.

Why, I think 'tis like a fine Lady; it looks best by Candle-Light.   10

MRS. HAZARD.

Mr. *Cross*, get every body ready; is the Music come?

MR. CROSS.

Yes, Madam, the Music has been here this half Hour, and every body but Mrs. *Clive*; and, I dare say, she'll not be long, for she's very punctual; Mr. *Beard* and Miss *Thomas* are gone to dress.   15

MRS. HAZARD.

Mr. *Cross*, you have had a great deal of Trouble with this Thing; I don't know how I must make you amends; but pray, when your Benefit is, – you have a Benefit, I suppose? – set me down all your Side-Boxes, and every first Row in the Front; I may want more; but I shall certainly fill those.   20

MR. CROSS.

Thank'ye, Madam.

Enter a Servant.

SERVANT.

Mr. *Cross*, there's a Person wants to speak to you.

Exit Mr. Cross.

MRS. HAZARD.

Well, I'll swear these poor Players have a very slavish Life; I wonder how they are able to go through it!

Enter Mr. Cross.

MR. CROSS.

Madam, Mrs. *Clive* has sent word, that she can't possibly 25
wait on you this Morning, as she's obliged to go to some Ladies about her Benefit. But you may depend on her being very perfect, and ready to perform it whenever you please.

MRS. HAZARD.

Mr. *Cross*, what did you say? I can't believe what I have heard! Mrs. *Clive* sent me word she can't come to my *Re-* 30
hearsal, and is gone to Ladies about her Benefit! Sir, she shall have no Benefit. Mr. *Witling*, did you ever hear of a Parallel to this Insolence? Give me my Copy, Sir; give me my Copy. I'll make Mrs. *Clive* repent treating me in this manner. Very fine indeed! to have the Assurance to prefer her Benefit to 35
my *Rehearsal*! Mr. *Cross*, you need not give yourself the Trouble to set down any Places for me at your Benefit, for I'll never come to the Play-house any more.

WITLING.

Nay; but my dear *Hazard*, don't put yourself into such a Passion; can't you rehearse her Part yourself? I dare say you'll do 40
it better than she can!

MR. CROSS.

Why, Madam, if you would be so good, as the Music are here, and the other Characters dressed, it would be very obliging: and if you please to put on Mrs. *Clive*'s Dress, her Dresser is here to attend, as she expected her, and I believe it 45
will fit you exactly, as you're much of her Size.

MRS. HAZARD.

O yes; to be sure it will fit me exactly, because I happen to be a Head taller, and I hope something better made.

WITLING.

Oh, my dear *Hazard*! put it on; put it on. Oh Lord! let me see you in a Play-house Dress. 50

MRS. HAZARD.

Well, let me die, but I have a great mind; – for I had set my Heart upon seeing the poor Thing rehearsed in its proper Dresses. – Well, *Witling*, shall I? – I think I will. Do you go into the Green Room and drink some Chocolate, I'll slip on the Things in a Minute. No; hang it, I won't take the   55 Trouble; I'll rehearse as I am.

Enter Performers dressed.

Miss *Thomas*, your Servant. Upon my Word, I am extremely happy to have you in my Performance; you'll do amazing well. Only I must beg you'd throw in as much Spirit as you can, without over-doing it; for that same Thing the Players   60 call *Spirit*, they sometimes turn into Rant and Noise. Oh, Mr. *Beard*! your most Obedient. Sir, I'll be vastly obliged to you, I am sure; do you know that you sing better than any of 'em? But I hope you'd consider the Part you are to act with *Marcella*, is to be done with great Scorn: therefore, as you   65 have such a smiling, good-humoured Face, I beg you'll en- deavour to smother as many of your Dimples as you can in that Scene with her. Come, come, let us begin. We may omit the Overture.

MIRANDA, [*Sola*.]

RECITATIVE.

It must be so – my Shepherd ne'er shall prove   70
A Renegado from the Faith of Love.
Nor shall Marcella *tear him from my Arms,*
Even tho' her Wealth be boundless as her Charms.

MRS. HAZARD.

That's pretty well, Madam, but I think you sing it too much; you should consider *Recitative* should be spoken as plain as   75 possible; or else you'll lose the Expression. – I'll shew you what I mean. – No, no, go on now with the Symphony for the Song.

AIR.

If Cupid *once the Mind possess,*
All low Affections cease;   80

No Troubles then can give distress,
　　No Tumult break the Peace.
Oh had I thousand Gifts in Store,
　　Were I of Worlds the Queen,
For him I'd covet thousands more,　　　　　85
　　And call Profusion mean.

2 .

Then let my Swain my Love return,
　　And equal Raptures feel;
Nor let his Passions cool, or burn,
　　As Fortune winds her Wheel.　　　　　90
If his fond Heart I may believe
　　Immutably secure,
No Sorrow then can make me grieve,
　　No Loss can make me poor.

RECITATIVE.

But see he comes – I'll wear a short Disguise;　　　95
Be false my Tongue! – be Hypocrites my Eyes!
Nor to the Youth too wantonly impart
The secret History of a faithful Heart.

Enter Corydon.

What! from Marcella come! – Insulting Swain,
Come ye to wake, and triumph in my Pain,　　　100
Warm from those Lips whose cruel Sentence gave
Thy Friend Philander an untimely Grave?

RECITATIVE.
CORYDON.

Marcella! name not the capricious Fair,
One Smile from thee is worth Possession there.
MIRANDA.

Did not I hear her in yon Hawthorn Bower　　　105
With Transport boast o'er Corydon her Power?

AIR.

CORYDON.

In vain, my Fair One, you complain,
And charge the guiltless Boy in vain,
 Who ne'er was found untrue;
The sweetest Image Thought can find,   110
Thou best Idea of my Mind,
 My Soul is fill'd with you.

2.

Let but those Eyes, benignly bright,
That look the Language of Delight,
 This spacious Globe review;   115
If they can find an equal Fair,
Be jealous then – and I'll take care
 You shall have reason too.

MIRANDA.

Well – wou'd you ease my Breast, and Peace restore,
Oh never see the vain Marcella more.   120

DUET.

AIR.

MIRANDA.

At length return luxuriant Thought,
Return and settle where you ought
Fix'd by Experience dearly bought
 For sweet and useful ends.
Oft did I dread her subtle Care,   125
And oft was jealous, tho' secure,
What Agonies did I endure?
 But Love has made amends.

CORYDON.

Joy were no Joy, and Pleasure vain,
Were there not Intervals of Pain;   130
The Captive who has felt a Chain
 Is doubly blest when free.
I view with Transports the Abyss,
Which Powers propitious made me miss,
And rush with aching Thoughts of Bliss   135

To Safety, and to thee.

BOTH.

Joy were no Joy, and Pleasure vain,
Were there not Intervals of Pain;
The Captive who has felt a Chain
Is doubly blest when free.   140
'Tis Clouds that make the Sun more bright,
'Tis Darkness that sets off the Light,
'Tis Sorrow gives to Joy its Height,
By Heaven's most kind Decree.

[Witling *falls asleep.*]

CORYDON.

Soft! she approaches — seek yon poplar Glade,   145
And wait beneath the thick embowering Shade.
Yourself shall be a Witness to my Truth.

Miranda *retires.*

Enter Marcella.

Oh Corydon, *ah cruel charming Youth,*
Look not so stern, I have no hopes to blast;
My Love is come in Sighs to breathe its last.   150

AIR.

The silver Rain, the pearly Dew,
The Gales that sweep along the Mead,
The soften'd Rocks have Sorrow knew,
And Marbles have found Tears to shed;
The sighing Trees, in every Grove,   155
Have Pity, if they have not Love.

2.

Shall things inanimate be kind,
And every soft Sensation know;
The weeping Rain, and sighing Wind,
All, all, but thee, some Mercy show.   160
Ah pity — if you scorn t'approve;

Have Pity, if thou hast not Love.

[*A Noise without.*]

Enter Miss Giggle, Sir Albany Odelove,
Miss Sidle, *and Miss* Dawdle.

MISS GIGGLE.

My dear Creature, I immensely rejoice to find you; do you
know we have been at your House, and could not meet with
a Creature that could give the least account of you? Your   165
Servants are all abroad, ha, ha, ha; they are certainly the
worst Servants in the World, ha, ha, ha. Well but my Dear,
have you done? for we must have you with us. We are going
to one of the breakfasting Places, but we don't know which
yet, for they are all so immensely superb, that I can't touch   170
my Breakfast at home, ha, ha, ha! Lord, dear Creature, what
makes you look so miserable? Your new thing isn't a Tragedy, is it?

MRS. HAZARD.

Giggle, I'm astonished at you: pray who are all these People
you have brought upon me? –   175

MISS GIGGLE.

Who are they my Dear? I'll introduce you to them; they're
immensely agreeable, all of them, ha, ha, ha.

MRS. HAZARD.

Lookee, Miss *Giggle,* if they are ever so immense, they must
not stay here, for I'm going to be immensely busy, and will
not be interrupted.   180

MISS GIGGLE.

My dear Creature, as to leaving you, 'tis not in the nature of
things; I would not go without you for all the World; Sir
Anthony Odelove, Mrs. *Hazard,* desires to be introduced to
you. Madam, this Gentleman is immensely fond of the
Muses, and therefore must be agreeable to you. Miss *Sidle,*   185
Miss *Dawdle* – [*Introduces 'em.*]

MRS. HAZARD [*Aside*].

Mr. *Cross,* – I want to speak to you; I shall run mad.

MISS GIGGLE.

Lord *Witling*, what's the matter with Mrs. *Hazard*? She looks
as if she could kill me.

WITLING.

The matter with her? ha, ha, ha! why, you have interrupted   190
her Rehearsal. Ah, I could indulge such a Laugh! If you'll
join with me, we shall have the finest Scene in the World. –
She has made me sick to death with her Stuff, and I will be
revenged. You must know one of the Actresses has disappointed her, and she is going to sing her Part herself; so the   195
Moment she begins, do you burst into a violent Laugh; and
we shall all join with you, you may be sure; and then you'll
see the Consequence. –

MISS GIGGLE.

See! nay, I believe I shall feel the Consequence, for she'll
certainly beat us immensely. Oh, I'll tell you what; let's set   200
Odelove upon her to enquire into the Plot of her Play. – He'll
plague her to death, for he's immensely foolish.

WITLING.

Well – that's an admirable Thought. – Mum. –

MISS GIGGLE.

Well, but my Dear Mrs. *Hazard*, don't let us interrupt you,
for we are all immensely fond of a Rehearsal.   205

MISS DAWDLE.

Yes, so we are indeed, Madam, immensely.

WITLING.

So we are, immensely. [*Catches her Hand.*]

MISS DAWDLE.

Lord! don't paw one so, Mr. *Witling*. –

MISS GIGGLE.

And so this is the Playhouse; I'll swear 'tis immensely pretty,
and all the Music; well, if there was but a Scene of green   210
Trees, we might fancy ourselves at *Ranelagh*, ha, ha, ha.

MRS. HAZARD.

Why really by the Noise you make, and the Nonsense you
talk, I think you might. Lookee, Miss *Giggle*, I shall be very

---

211 *Ranelagh*] A more fashionable rival to Vauxhall Gardens, Ranelagh stood on
the north side of the Thames, in Chelsea. Ranelagh's main feature was a
rotunda where fashionable crowds could dance, mingle, and promenade.

plain with you; if you think it is possible for you to be quiet for half an Hour, I shall be glad of your Company; if not, I must beg you'd depart. 215

SIR ALBANY.

Why really what the Lady says, is very pathetic and consequential to the foregoing Part of Miss *Giggle*'s Behaviour; for when a Person of Parts, (as we are to suppose this Lady to be) is assassinated with Incoherences, it is such an Aggravation to our Intellects, as does in fact require supernatural Patience to acquiesce thereto. 220

ALL.

Ha! ha! ha!

MISS GIGGLE.

Very well, Sir *Albany*, I'll remember you for this. – No, upon Honour, now I will be very good, I won't interrupt you indeed, won't speak another Word. – O la, *Witling*, do you know that Miss *Lucy Loveshuffle* had such an immense ill Run last Night, she bragged everything that came into her Hand, and lost everything she bragged – 'till she really looked as ugly as a Fiend. 225

230

WITLING.

I fancy you won then, *Giggle*: for I never saw you look so well.

MRS. HAZARD.

Nay as to that matter, let *Giggle* win, or lose, it will be pretty much the same things with her Beauty; but come, Mr. *Cross*, pray let us go on. Let me see, I'll begin my Recit. 235

SIR ALBANY.

Corydon. –

WITLING.

Giggle, I can tell you who's going to be married.

MISS SIDLE AND MISS DAWDLE.

Oh Lord! who? – pray tell us?

WITLING.

The celebrated Miss *Shrimp* to Lord *Lovelittle*, a Man of very great Fortune. 240

MISS DAWDLE.

Really! Well then, I think we none of us need to despair.

WITLING.

> Come, don't you be envious now; for she's a charming Girl, and deserves her good Fortune.

MISS GIGGLE.

> Charming! – nay then I shall never have done, I'm sure she's immensely little. 245

SIR ALBANY.

> Oh fy Miss, that's Nonsense; horrid Nonsense! immensely little! Oh Lord!

WITLING.

> Why, to be sure she is rather small, that must be allowed; she is certainly the least Woman that ever was seen for nothing.

SIR ALBANY.

> Madam, as I was not so auspicious as to be here at the beginning of this Affair, will you give me leave to ask you a few 250 Questions? –

MR. CROSS.

> Madam, if you won't go on, the Music and Performers can't possibly stay any longer.

MRS. HAZARD.

> Why what can I do, Mr. *Cross*? You see how I'm terrified 255 with 'em.

WITLING.

> She begins to be in a fury. – Look at her, *Giggle*.

SIR ALBANY.

> I say, Madam, will you give me leave, as you're going to entertain the Town, (that is, I mean, to endeavour, or to attempt to entertain them) for let me tell you, fair Lady, 'tis 260 not an easy thing to bring about. If Men, who are properly graduated in Learning, who have swallowed the Tincture of a polite Education, who, as I may say, are hand and glove with the Classics, if such Geniuses as I'm describing, fail of Success in Dramatical Occurrences, or Performances, ('tis 265 the same Sense in the Latin) what must a poor Lady to expect, who is ignorant as the Dirt.

MRS. HAZARD.

> Pray Sir, how long have they let you out?

SIR ALBANY.

> Therefore, I hope you have had the Advice of your Male Acquaintance, who will take some Care of your Diction, 270

and see that you have observed that great Beauty, neglected
by most Dramatic Authors, of Time and Place.

WITLING.

Oh Sir *Albany*, I'll answer she has taken care of Time and
Place; for it will begin about half an Hour after Eight; and be
acted at *Drury-Lane* Theatre. – Ha, ha, ha, there's Time and   275
Place for you.

MRS. HAZARD.

And so, you're hand and glove with the Classics, are you?
Why thou elaborate Idiot, how durst you venture to talk
about any thing that's Rational? – Consult my Male Ac-
quaintance! I thank my Stars, thou art not one of 'em.   280
Where did you pick up this Creature? – what's his Name? –
Can you spell your own Name, you ugly Brute?

MISS GIGGLE.

Oh Lord! it will never come to her Singing.

MISS SIDLE.

Pray Madam, will there be any Dancing this Morning?

MRS. HAZARD.

No. – Mr. *Cross*, who let these People in? I do assure you I   285
shall complain to the Managers; – I have been so plagued
there's no bearing it – I could tear these – I'm unfit for any
thing now. – So the Rehearsal must be put off, 'till another
Morning.

WITLING.

Ay do; – and let us go –   290

MRS. HAZARD.

Go to –

WITLING.

To *Ranelagh* – I knew you would not name an ungenteel
Place.

SIR ALBANY.

The Lady has been somewhat underbred in her Behaviour to
me; but as I have a Regard to the Fair Sex, I would have   295
some of you advise her to cry; it will give Relief to her Passion.

MRS. HAZARD.

Sir, will you go out of this Place?

SIR ALBANY.

I protest, Madam, I will, directly.

Exit.

ALL.

Ha, ha, ha! 300

WITLING.

Well, but my dear Creature, you are not angry with me? –

MRS. HAZARD.

Indeed I am, *Witling*, and very angry too; I don't believe I
shall ever speak to you again. As for those Things, that run
about littering the Town, and force themselves into all public Places only to shew their Insignificance, they are beneath 305
my Resentment. – Mr. *Cross*, I'll settle with you, when I
would have another Rehearsal; tho' I am not sure I ever will
have another. – I believe I shall tear it to Pieces. – Pray let
somebody see if my Chairmen are there.

WITLING.

Shall I wait on you? 310

MRS. HAZARD.

No.

Exit.

WITLING.

Well, as Sir *Paul* says, Odsbud, she's a passionate Woman;
but her tearing it, will only save the Audience the Trouble of
doing it for her. Come, Ladies, will you go? I'll see you to
your Coach. 315

MR. CROSS.

As the Ladies have been disappointed of Mrs. *Hazard*'s Rehearsal, if they please to stay, we are going to practice a new
Dance.

ALL.

Oh, by all Means.

A DANCE.

FINIS

Textual Notes

The Clandestine Marriage

The text is based on the first edition, published by T. Becket and P.A. De Hondt, 1766. Five printings of the play were published in 1766, which Pedicord and Bergmann list as five separate editions. Generally, all five "editions" agree in their readings, but there are some important departures, especially in Act III. I have consulted a copy of the second edition – which I refer to as the British Museum Copy – and compared alternate readings with that of the first edition. It is impossible to say with any certainty which text is closer to the play in performance, but the cuts and alterations are so slight that both texts – or even a composite – may have been performed on any given night.

I have also compared the 1766 printings with later editions, particularly *The Dramatic Works of George Colman* (1777) and the posthumous *Dramatic Works of David Garrick* (1798), which make significant changes in spelling and punctuation. Some of the changes represent changes in spelling fashion – e.g. "music" for "musick" – but most of the alterations attempt to "normalise" Mrs. Heidelberg's dialect speech, so that much of the flavour of her character is lost when spellings such as "quality" and "family" are substituted for her more characteristic "qualaty" and "fammaly." I have retained Mrs. Heidelberg's unusual pronounciations throughout.

I have also retained the punctuation of the 1766 printings, even where the punctuation would seem illogical or incorrect to a modern reader. Garrick and Colman saw their plays through to press, and the punctuation of the earliest editions provides clues to the way the dialogue was originally spoken. In particular, the large number of dashes that litter the first editions indicate significant pauses in speech. Similarly, rhetorical questions are often punctuated with an exclamation mark, indicating that the inflection called for is not that of a sincere question, but of surprise or astonishment. The difference between "What?" and "What!" on stage can be significant. I have compared the speech-rhythms in the 1766 edition with Pedicord and Bergmann's modernised edition, and have found that modernisation of the punctuation often suggests a different interpretation of the whole line. Rather than risk such interpretation myself, I have left the punctuation much as it is. However, I have supplied periods before dashes when the word following begins with a capital (a practice inconsistently followed in the original); I have also regularised the punctuation and capitalisation of stage-directions.

I have left the spelling unmodernised except in a few specific cases:

(i) "'d" has been expanded to "ed" throughout, except in the Prologue and Epilogue; similarly, contracted forms such as "cou'd" and "shou'd," which only occasionally appear, have been expanded to "could" and "should."

(ii) words such as "to-morrow" and "to-night" are printed as "tomorrow" and "tonight."

(iii) the few obvious printing errors in the original have been silently corrected.

Finally, I should note that Pedicord and Bergmann's text, though useful for providing a record of the various editions printed in Garrick's lifetime along with many of the variant readings, is littered with errors and infidelities of its own. Pedicord and Bergmann often alter words that have no authority in any of the early printings; they are guilty of obvious misreadings (such as "insure" for "ensure"); finally, they provide no guide to the reader of their editorial practices. The inadequacies of this edition as a scholarly text of Garrick's plays has been noted by Leo Hughes ("A Flawed Tribute to Garrick." *Modern Philology* 80.4, 398-405).

Copies Consulted:

Yale:
First edition, octavo, published by T. Becket and P.A. DeHondt, 1766. Copy-text for present edition. The copy held by Yale University is generally recognised as the first printing, issued shortly after the first performance in February, 1766.

British Museum:
A second octavo, published the same year. The British Museum copy shows some signs of revision, particularly in the lawyer scene in Act III. Variants are noted below.

1770:
"A New Edition," also published by Becket and DeHondt. A.E.

Morgan speculates that the revisions are primarily by Colman. The 1770 edition generally follows the British Museum additions and revisions, and incorporates new readings of its own. In general, the 1770 edition makes the language less colloquial, and normalises Mrs. Heidelberg's idiosyncratic spelling.

1777:
In *The Dramatic Works of George Colman*. This text contains a significant number of revisions, and incorporates many of the British Museum and 1770 readings. The revisions are almost certainly Colman's, and continues the process of regularisation begun in 1770.

Advertisement

    7-15   In Justice...CLANDESTINE MARRIAGE] Some friends, and some enemies, have endeavoured to allot distinct portions of this play to each of the Authors. Each, however, considers himself responsible for the whole; and though they have, on other occasions, been separately honoured with the indulgence of the publick, it is with peculiar pleasure that they now make their joint acknowledgements for the very favourable reception of the *Clandestine Marriage*. Substituted in 1777.

Dramatis Personae
    Mrs. – .] Mrs. Abington 1777.

I.i

    3   I'm] I am 1770.
    52   loviers] *loviers* 1777.
    55   say so] say 1777.
    128   Quality] quality 1777.
    216   will] would 1770.
    239   an] a 1770.
    240   Well – well] Well 1777.
    256   Lordship] lordship 1777.

I.ii

    16   Lovewell, Sister?] BM, 1770, 1777; Lovewell? Sister! Yale.

54 snug wig] smug wig Yale, BM 1770, 1777. Corrected in *Dramatic Works of David Garrick*, 1798.

70 father] 1770, 1777; farther Yale, BM.

113 shamb] chamb 1770

117 ye] you 1777

119 possible] possable 1770

121 immediately.] immediately. And set them o'nodding as soon as his lordship comes in, d'ye hear, Trusty? 1777.

140 opportunity] opportoonity 1770.

162 politeness] puliteness 1770.

190 Mons. Cantoon] mounseer Cantoon 1777.

212 at least, I'm] at least; that I am 1777.

II.i

75 de Deviel] the Deviel 1770.

131 little] like 1770; litt 1777.

s.d. (*Giving the surfeit-water*)] 1777; not in Yale, BM, 1770.

155 it is] is it Yale, BM, 1770, 1777. Lord Ogleby's remark here seems to me more of a statement than a question, hence the editorial alteration.

179 *Aside*] not in Yale, BM, 1770, 1777.

206-7 go the Grand Tower] go to the Grand Tower Yale, BM.

215 under] into 1770.

218 spirits] spirit 1777

230 Sterling] Steerling 1777 (misprint?)

234 *Aloud*] not in Yale, BM, 1770, 1777.

236 shall have 'em] shall have them 1777.

II.ii

7 Where was] Where were 1777.

12 where was] where were 1777.

33 grisette] om. 1777.

64 gothic] gothick BM, 1770, 1777.

94 doats] dotes 1777.

146 You was] You were 1777.

167 Her] her 1770, 1777.

181 true – but] true. But BM.

194	Why that – that is] Why that – is 1770.
220	encouragement] *encouragement* 1777.
225	surprise] surprize 1770, 1777.
226	surprised] surprized 1770, 1777.
282	your's] yours 1770.

III.i

5	names, gentlemen] names. 1770.
6	two BM, 1770, 1777] three Yale. Apparently a misprint since only three characters in total appear here.
17	Midland, Oxford, and Western] Midland and Western BM, 1770, 1777.
19	Abingdon] Hertford BM, 1770, 1777.
28	True, Mr. Serjeant.] Yale; True, Mr Serjeant – and the easiest thing in the world too – for those country attornies are such ignorant dogs, that in the case of the devise of an estate to A. and his heirs for ever, they'll make a query, whether he takes in fee or in tail. BM, 1770, 1777
85	60,000 l.] sixty thousand pounds 1777.
89	80,000 l.] eighty thousand pounds 1777.
100	2000 l.] two thousand pounds 1777.
104	thousands] thousand 1777.
111–12	We'll have no jolts...new pavement] om. BM, 1770.
128-29	in the green] on the green BM, 1770.
178	daughters] daughter 1770, 1777.
186	of disrespect] of any disrespect 1770.
194	I do not] I don't 1770.
241	transfer] transfer your addresses 1777.
255	niece] BM, 1770; neice Yale.
262	(*going*)] om. BM, 1770.

III.ii.

6	niece] BM, 1770; neice Yale.
18	Melville] Melvil 1777.
19	creepin] creppin 1770.
35	diffuring] diffurring 1777.
43	perfet] perfect 1770.

48	hand] hands 1770.
64	past] pass'd 1777.
70	past] pass'd 1777.
72	opinon] opinion 1770.
74	quallaty] qualaty 1770, 1777.
92	monstrus] monstrous 1770.
119	fie for shame] fy for shame 1777.
163	Oh fie, Sir John!] Oh fy, Sir John! 1777.
164	indignaty] indignety 1777.
177	lawyers] counsellors 1770.
179	hundred] three hundred 1770.
206	ballance] balance 1770, 1777.

IV.i.

4	Positively] Posatively 1770.
17	vigur] vigour 1777.
36	you must do] you shall do 1770.

IV.ii.

31	most] more 1770.
35	cephalick] cephalic 1777.
49	enjouée] enjoué 1770; *enjoué* 1777.
62–63	It will come] It would come 1777.
85	fixt] fix'd 1777.
103–4	de *poor pigeone*] the *poor pigeone* 1770.
141	father] family 1770.
163	you to do him the honour] you do him de honeur 1770, 1777.
163	little] litt 1777.
s.d.	(*manent Lord Ogleby and Sterling*)] 1777; not in Yale, BM, 1770.
242	exquisite feelings] feeling 1770.
432	go and] om. 1770.

V.ii.

50	protest] pertest 1777.
77–78	what d'ye call 'em] What-d'ye-call-em's 1770.
90	Rats, I suppose] Rats! Rats, I suppose 1777.
111	you, to say] you to say 1770.
190	whole family] whole famaly 1770, 1777.

220	this tintamarre] dis tintamarre 1770.
238	ladies' making] 1777; ladies making Yale, BM.
274	creatures] creaturs 1777.
320	cares are lost] cares were lost 1770.
360	ballance] balance 1777.

Epilogue

The Musick by Mr. Barthelemon] 1777; not in Yale, BM, 1770.

Miss Mills] Miss Pearce 1777.

16	the odd] th'odd 1777.
33	Jonsons] 1777; Johnsons Yale, BM, 1770.
61	Light] Lights 1770.

The Cunning-Man

The text is based on the second edition, published by Becket and De Hondt (1766). This edition records changes made to the text after the first performance, and includes a note of thanks from Burney to the managers and performers at Drury Lane. The text has been collated with Bell's British Theatre edition, the only other major eighteenth-century edition.

Copies Consulted:

1766:
Second edition, published by T. Becket and P.A. DeHondt. The second edition is generally regarded as the best text, since it represents Burney's revisions prepared for the November 21 premiere at Drury Lane. Burney also indicated the cuts made in the performance.

1784:
Bell's British Theatre edition. The texts prepared by John Bell for his series of contemporary British plays are generally authoritative. Bell was a friend of Garrick's, and had access to the promptbooks and other material at Drury Lane. This text follows the Second Edition, with a few minor emendations.

Advertisement] om. 1784

I.i

    9   Nymph] nymph 1784.
    9   Fair] fair 1784.
    19   ought,] ought: 1784.
    22   Why then for ever] Why, then, for ever 1784.
    24   foretell] foretel 1784.

I.ii

         SCENE II] om. 1784.
    s.d. *Enter Cunning-Man*] 1784; not in 1766.
    s.d. Paper,] paper 1784
    2   Tell me,] Tell me 1784.
    5   asswage] assuage 1784.
    8   you] you: 1784.
    12   Ye?] Ye! 1784.
    19   Rover] rover 1784.
    40   Love] love 1784.
    49   him,] him; 1784.

I.iii

         SCENE III] om. 1784.

I.iv

         SCENE IV] om. 1784.
    s.d. *Enter Colin*] 1784; not in 1766.
    2   now, for Phœbe,] now for Phœbe 1784.
         AIR] om. 1784.
    14   Lord] lord 1784.
    s.d. *Conjuring-book*] *conjuring book* 1784.

I.v

         SCENE V] om. 1784
    2   will aid –] will aid 1784.
    3   Lovers] lovers 1784.
    7   Goods] goods 1784.
    8   Hearts] hearts 1784.
    14   mystery] myst'ry 1784.
    17   Fortune] fortune 1784.

II.i

1	Nymph] nymph 1784.
11	Maid] maid 1784.
13	oaten] 1784; oaken 1766.

II.ii

	SCENE II] om. 1784
s.d.	*Enter Phœbe*] 1784; not in 1766.
14	sagacious,] sagacious 1784.
31	*To Colin*] om. 1784.
38	– What?] – What? – 1784.
40	woe] wo 1784.
44	name:] name. 1784.
60	goods] 1784; good 1766.
64	profer'd] proffer'd 1784.
65	Ah!] Ah, 1784.
66	Ah!] Ah, 1784
s.d.	*ribband*] *riband* 1784.

II.iii

SCENE III] om. 1784

II.iv

	SCENE IV] om. 1784
6	sing] sing, 1784.
42	Though] Tho' 1784.
104	musick] music 1784.

The Rehearsal; Or Bays in Petticoats

The text is based on the first printed edition of 1753. As the advertisement notes, this text is a revision of the afterpiece as it was performed in 1750, and contains an additional scene not in the manuscript, preserved in the Larpent Collection. I have chosen the 1753 edition as Clive's final extant version of the play: the additions and alterations made to the 1755 performances do not appear to be extant.

I have modernised the text following the same principles as *The Clandestine Marriage*.

Appendix A:Contemporary Reviews

1. The Clandestine Marriage

London Magazine, February 1766, 63-4.

The *Clandestine Marriage*, which there was some reason to apprehend would have remained still in secret, is now publicly known; and from the ablest opinions, we are assured, that it will stand firm and good in critic law.

Prologues and epilogues are a sort of master to the ceremonies, appointed by custom, to introduce a dramatic author to a public audience, for presenting his credentials and taking leave. They are in fact no more essential to the play itself, than the title-page and finis to a book; and Dryden has complained, not without reason, of the trouble it gave him, to furnish these ornamental head and tail pieces to the drama. In the prologue to the Clandestine Marriage there is, however, a most happy use made of the temporary occasion to drop

> "　　　　　　　　———— a tributary Tear
> On poor Jack Falstaff's Grave, and Juliet's Bier!"

In the beginning no less honour is paid to the memory of Hogarth; and we are made acquainted, that the author of the play had the same object in view with the painter, viz. to represent marriage à la Mode, though their story and characters are not the same. The epilogue is, indeed, very different from what we have been used to see, – a lady tripping in with a simpering smile, and then curtseying all round, with an officious whisperer behind her. It is rather a *postlude*, or after-play, representing an assemblage of polite people over their card-tables at a modern rout, who furnish an odd mixed conversation-piece, with singing into the bargain; and, in truth, there is too much tweedle-dum and tweedle-dee in it.

As to the play we shall not attempt to point out the excellencies of the plot, characters, diction, &c. till it appears in print. We beg, in the mean time, leave to advise Mr. King, (who otherwise sustains, with great propriety, the character of an old, battered, conceited beau of a nobleman, that fancies every woman admires him,) not to appear with so cadaverous a countenance in his first scene, or with so very grim and horrid an aspect afterwards. The lawyers too may as well make some abridgement of their jargon, as it is none of the most intelligible. We would also advise the managers to be at the expence of a few lights, to be brought on after a while in the last act, as a signal for the lamps to rise. We are of opinion likewise, that Miss Sterling and Mrs. Heidelburgh [sic], should be less frequent and vociferous in their bawling out *thieves! thieves!* – as we are certain, that had this play been acted at Covent Garden, such a violent noise would have excited the vigilance of a neighbouring magistrate.

Upon the whole it is but justice to acknowledge, that this piece is not unworthy of the Author of *The Jealous Wife* [i.e. George Colman]. The Fable is extremely interesting, it abounds with sprightly sallies of wit; the incidents are well contrived, the characters are strongly marked, and the language is remarkably pure, easy and elegant: And as almost the whole strength of the company was employed in the performance, it is no wonder that the representation met with such universal applause.

Francis Gentleman, The Dramatic Censor; Or, Critical Companion. 2 Vols. (london, 1770): I:239-55.

We have either observed, or meant to observe, that spirit and propriety of character, vivacity of dialogue, wit, and variety of incidents, are the constituent parts of a good comedy; many of late have got into the stile of mere sentiment, and chit-chat picked up from novels, which they are vain and idle enough to suppose compleat dramas; if such authors are right, Ben Jonson, Wycherley, Congreve, Farquhar and Cibber, were undoubtedly wrong; licenciousness, 'tis true, has disappeared, but in general it seems as if wit and pleasantry, who were too long united with so bad a companion, had followed their old ally; how far the child of poetical partnership now before us has fallen into or avoided the fashionable languor let candid consideration declare.

[Gentleman recounts the entire plot act by act, pausing occasionally to offer comments on the characters or the structure of the play. For example, at the opening of Act II he remarks:]

Nothing can be more happily imagined, or better conducted than the introduction of Lord Ogleby, whose figure and manners make irresistible appeals to laughter; nor is the Swiss sycophant Canton any way unequal to the ennobled oddity, his master; Canton's insinuation that both the Miss Sterlings seem attached to his Lordship, is not only a fine attack on the peer's weak side, but works up Ogleby to a most ludicrous opinion of his influence amongst the ladies; the merchant's praise of the accommodation his house affords, and his intention of hurrying the feebled peer from one spot to another, for sake of viewing what he presumes tasteful improvements, keeps up the dialogue with much pleasantry.

[Gentleman is more critical of the Sir John/Lovewell scene that preceeds Sterling's tour of the garden (II.ii.135-273):]

The ensuing unfinished scene between Sir John Melville and Lovewell, seems a mere excrescence, the lopping off which would make no gap nor any way mutilate the piece; in that between my lord, the merchant, Mrs. Heidelberg, and the two young ladies, we apprehend Sterling's clumsiness of taste is rather too much displayed; the humour seems to confess a strain upon that point, but takes an agreeable turn when his lordship's vanity interprets the present of a nosegay from Fanny as love, and that of another from Miss Sterling as jealousy; the silent situation of Sir John and Lovewell through so long a scene, might, and undoubtedly should have been avoided; for though Sir John's explanation affords some little grounds for action in Lovewell, when he finds the baronet's affection placed on his wife; yet the conversation is much too long for what it turns upon, and rather damps that spirit which happily enlivens most other parts of this piece.

[Of the Lord Ogleby/Fanny scene in Act IV (IV.ii.95-216), Gentleman remarks:]

There is a very artful and regular climax of humour, which rises with every fresh character, and keeps the peer, for an usual length of dialogue, so far from palling that even at the end of the act, we wish for more of him; his triumph over Sir John's pretensions to Fanny gives a most agreeable variation of pleasantry, and we are doubtful if any dramatic character was ever better supported so long together.

[Finally, Gentleman comments on the play in performance:]

The language of this piece is spirited, and in general chaste, though not elegant; the sentiments just without brilliance, the incidents well ranged, the plot pleasingly unfolded, judiciously conducted, and well wrought up to the catastrophe: as to wit, it traces natural conversation of the present day so close, as not to have a spark throughout the five acts; and for moral, it has not the shadow of one, which the authors seemed conscious of, when, instead of advertising so essential a point, they adopted the pitiful, though classical, mode of conclusion by begging applause from the audience; which is a little like Merry-Andrew's bidding *his* audience shout, when he has played tricks before them: in an epilogue, such a sugar-sop may be dropped to sweeten the acidity of critical opinion; but at the end of a play, it must certainly be deemed a piece of poetical sycophantism.

Lord Ogleby, though pronounced a very near relation of lord Chalkestone [i.e. Garrick's celebrated character in *Lethe*], is most certainly as much an original, and as much a child of laughter, as any character on the stage – harmlessly vain, pleasantly odd, commendably generous; a coxcomb not void of sense, a master full of whim, a lover full of false fire, yet a valuable friend; possessed of delicate feelings and nice honour; the peculiarities of this difficult part are supported with eminent abilities by that most excellent comedian Mr. KING, who notwithstanding his chief praise derives from being a chaste delineator of nature, here strikes out in the water colour painting of life, a most beautiful and striking caricature, conceived with some degree of poetical extravagance, yet so meliorated by his execution, that thousands who have never seen such a human being as Lord Ogleby, must, amidst involuntary bursts of laughter, allow, nay wish there may be such a man, whose foibles are so inoffensive.

If Mr. KING shews more merit in any one passage than another, it is where Sterling says to the young couple "Lovewell, you shall leave my house; and, madam, you shall follow him;" [V.ii.366, slightly misquoted] to which the peer with infinite good nature replies, "and if they do, I shall receive them into mine." [V.ii.368] – Though it does not always follow that what an actor feels most he can express best; yet we may venture to say a kind of sympathetic union gives this short sentence peculiar force and beauty in Mr. KING's utterance.

Sir John Melville is the chief confusion-maker of the piece, of so indifferent principles and insipid qualifications; ease and gentility of deportment, which are the only requisites necessary for this gentleman, were equally wanting in the late Mr. HOLLAND, and the present Mr. AICKIN: however, tolerable propriety is as much as this water-gruel baronet deserves, and so far he received no injury from these gentlemen.

Sterling is a well drawn uniform character, mounted upon the stilts of property, aiming at and boasting of taste he has not: grappling at pelf of which he has a superfluity; selfish and positive, where he dare exercise authority; ostentatious, methodical and ignorant; thus compounded he gives considerable life to those scenes where he is concerned, when assisted by Mr. YATES's inimitable talents for such characters; but in the hands of Mr. LOVE sinks beneath criticism, and seems only calculated to lull attention to sleep; it is a great pity this monotonous gentleman rose any higher than Serjeant FLOWER; the florid unvarying importance of physiognomy he commonly wears, being better adapted to a lumber headed lawyer, than any other character.

Lovewell engages an audience by his tender sentiments, and affectionate sincerity; his situation affects, and his manners please us; Mr. POWELL never made a more agreeable figure in comedy, nor perhaps so good a one as this part, which being placed in a station of life that he himself filled not long before; and being happily suited not only to his external appearance, but his internal feelings also, he satisfied most agreeably every point of expectation; ever Mr. CAUTHERLY, though far beneath the original, is not an insufferable Lovewell.

The lawyers are drawn in a masterly manner, and for the reason assigned above, we think Mr. LOVE had merit in the Serjeant – would he had never been removed; however, it must be allowed that Mr. BRANSBY is a worthy successor, as he supports at least the *weight* of the character with equal merit.

Canton is an admirable delineation of a foreign sycophant playing upon a vain English nobleman; the picture is instructive, and held to view in a very just advantageous point of light by Mr. BADDELEY, who breaks expression well in the Swiss Dialect, and cringes through the part in a very characteristic manner.

Brush is an excellent contrast of the assuming English valet, and while in view, claims some notice – the late Mr. PALMER deserved and met more applause than could be expected to attend so short a character, where tipsey he was highly laughable; his successor and name-sake if not quite so pleasant; has nevertheless a considerable share of merit.

As Farquhar said in respect of Sir Harry Wildair, that when Mr. WILKS died or left the stage he might really go to the jubilee; so without exaggeration we may say that Mrs. Heidelberg was lost to the public when Mrs. CLIVE retired; the ignorant affectation, volubility of expression, and happy disposition of external appearance, she was so remarkable for, will render it difficult to find an equivalent; in many characters she proved herself mistress of a fund of laughter, but was in none more luxuriantly droll than this, every line of the author was very becomingly enforced, and many passages were much improved by emphatic illustration, in such undertakings we have never seen her equal, and doubt if ever we may, Mrs. HOPKINS is scarce a shadow of her.

Miss Sterling, a character quite unfinished, says a good deal to very little purpose, is eat up with ambition, and I am afraid, with envy: she seems to have no commendable principles about her, her first scene indeed exhibits a considerable share of harmless spirit though what follows rather speaks malevolence.

She is left at the catastrophe in a most undetermined, and we may add, notwithstanding her foibles, an unsatisfactory state; the authors have made something of her at first, to drop her into nothing at last; in this view, she must rather be a dead weight upon any performer; however, Miss POPE, surmounting disadvantages, renders the young lady rather more than tolerable.

Fanny has a manifest advantage of her sister in simplicity of manners, disinterestedness of affection, and delicacy of feeling; her situation also happily enforces the amiable parts of her character; Mrs. PALMER, the original in this part, spoke more both to the head and heart, than Mrs. BADDELEY either does or can do; some lucky hits, with a more pleasing figure, make her pass off upon general opinion as well as her predecessor, but where criticism interferes, we must think much more favourably of the past than the present.

Betty will never again be performed with merit equal to the lady, who with much justice declined the insertion of her name in the drama for so insignificant a character; a character far below her capabilities, almost as far as it is above Mrs. LOVE's execution, of whom it was literally cruel to make an actress – yet by some accountable fatality, this unhappy lady is shoved on for many things, which would have been much better in other hands, and could not be worse in any. – Why, why will managers so far mistake the judgment of an audience, as to venture the intrusion of such creatures as understand little, and express less.

The chambermaid, according to what is said of her, was as well figured and played as ever she will be, by Miss PLYMM.

To speak of the piece in a complicate view, it certainly has a great deal of acting merit – a thorough knowledge of life and character is essential to draw comic scenes successfully; of this the CLANDESTINE MARRIAGE is a pleasing proof; however, some of the scenes are heavy, and a few trifling; the dialogue is not so spirited and easy as Farquhar's, nor so luxuriant and nervous as Congreve's, yet agreeably disengaged; the satire well pointed, and the sentiments lively, though not generally instructive: if standing the test of closet criticism be the fairest and most estimable degree of merit, we must not venture to place this piece among the foremost; but in representation, we are willing to allow it every point of approbation, which the indulgent public has favoured it with, and much more than many others can claim, which possess those very requisites the CLANDESTINE MARRIAGE wants.

2. *The Cunning-Man*

Gentleman's Magazine, *November 1766 (36.11), 543.*

This is a translation of a petit piece, called *Le Devin du Village*, the words and music of which are by the celebrated *J.J. Rousseau*.

The translator has adapted his translation to the melodies that were made to the *French* words and measure, with so little violence to our language, that he does not appear to have been under any restraint. It has not any concatenation of events that may be called a plot, but the dialogue is pleasing, the versification easy, and the tenor of the original, in many places, happily preserved.

[Not all accounts of the play were as favourable. The following excerpt is part of a general attack on the two theatres. Along with *The Cunning-Man* (the higher of the "two pot gun farces"), the poem refers to Garrick's tame adaptation of Wycherly's *The Country Wife*, and the afterpieces *Harlequin Dr. Faustus* and Garrick's own *Neck or Nothing*.]

Gentleman's Magazine, *January 1767 (37.1), 42*

"Upon the Performances exhibited at the two Theatres this Winter"

> Come, Madam justice, poize your scales
> That neither this, nor that prevails;
> And weigh with me, *Plays, Op'ras, Farces,*
> Nay, *Pantomimes* in doggrel verses;
> And let us judge by what is past,
> How much this year excels the last:
> Of *Quantity* we've had enough,
> The *Quality* must mark the stuff.
>
> Imprimis – At Old Drury Royal
> Have they to *Shakespeare* been so loyal?
> They gave us for a charming piece,
> (But Poets *swans* are always *geese*)
> A *whore* of Wycherly's lewd pen
> Chang'd to a flabby *Magdalen*
> To answer this at t'other house,
> The mountain labour'd with a mouse.
> What money, patience, time it cost us,
> To see dull plays, with duller *Faustus*:
> At which, as wit with Drury scarce is,
> They fir'd at once two pot gun farces
> One was too *high*, and one too *low:*
> Buckhorse wrote this, and that *Rousseau*.

Appendix B: Notes On The Actors

ABINGTON, Frances (Mrs. James, née Burton) (1737-1815) – Betty (*Clandestine Marriage*); Miss Crotchet ("Epilogue")

Frances Abington began her career in 1725 at the Haymarket Theatre under Theophilus Cibber. Her debut role was Miranda in Susanna Centlivre's *Busy Body*. She was soon hired by Edward Shuter for summer performances at Bath and Richmond; by 1756 she was a permanent member of the Drury Lane company. In 1759 she married James Abington, a minor actor and King's Trumpeter. She left Garrick's company in the early 1760s to enjoy successful seasons in Dublin, returning in 1765 to Drury Lane with her role as Widow Belmour in Arthur Murphy's *The Way to Keep Him*. Abington became convinced that Garrick had established a cabal to ruin her career: she was so upset by her minor part in *The Clandestine Marriage* that she insisted her name be removed from the first printings. After Sheridan assumed management of Drury Lane matters were somewhat settled, but by 1782 Abington left to join Covent Garden.

AICKIN, Francis (d. 1805) – Trueman (*Clandestine Marriage*)

Francis Aickin was born in Dublin, elder brother of fellow Drury Lane performer James Aickin. Aickin abandoned his father's weaving-trade in 1754 to join an Irish acting troupe; his first major role was George Barnwell in Lillo's tragedy. He left Ireland in 1765 and was immediately hired by Garrick. He remained at Drury Lane until 1774, where he established a specialty in villainous characters: his nickname was "Tyrant Aickin." For unknown reasons, Aickin was dismissed from the troupe. He moved to Covent Garden and continued his successful career, supplementing his regular season with summer work at the Haymarket. In later years, Aickin managed a theatre in Liverpool, which he initially renovated, but soon let fall into disrepair.

ARNE, Elizabeth (née Wright) (1751-1769) – Phœbe (*Cunning-Man*)

Probably born in 1751, Elizabeth Wright seems to have come

from an acting family. Her first stage appearance was at Drury Lane in 1761, as a fairy in *Edgar and Emmeline*. She also appeared in a revival of the Burney/Woodward pantomime, *Queen Mab*. In November, 1766 she married Michael Arne, son of composer Thomas Augustine Arne. Throughout her short life she appeared in numerous light operatic roles; she was often praised for the sweetness of her voice. However, she was easily overworked, and her health rapidly deteriorated. It is uncertain whether she reached her eighteenth birthday before she died.

BADDELEY, Robert (1733-1794) – Canton (*Clandestine Marriage*)
The role of Mons. Canton in *The Clandestine Marriage* seems to have been written with Robert Baddeley's particular talent for playing "national" characters in mind: Baddeley's specialties were Swiss, German and French types. Baddeley made his first stage appearance in 1760 at the Haymarket as Sir William Wealthy in Samuel Foote's *The Minor*. He made his debut at Drury Lane in the fall of the same year. Two paintings by theatre portrait artist Johann Zoffany show him in his celebrated role as Mons. Canton and as Moses in Sheridan's *School for Scandal*. Offstage, Baddeley was well known as a dandy: he spent fortunes on women and clothes. He eloped with Sophia Snow, a Drury Lane actress noted for her role as Fanny Sterling in *The Clandestine Marriage*, but the marriage was troubled by Baddeley's womanising and his jealousy. In 1770 he fought a bloodless duel with Garrick's brother George over Sophia that resulted in the couple's separation. Baddeley mentions two mistresses – Catherine Sherry and Catherine Strickland – in his will.

BEARD, John (1716-1791) – Corydon (*Bayes in Petticoats*)
Born in London, John Beard began his long musical career at the age of 15 as a boy treble in a special performance of Handel's *Esther* mounted as a birthday present for the composer. Later, Handel recognised the talents of this tenor, and composed numerous oratorio parts for him, including *Jeptha* and *Messiah*. Beard was also noted for his ballad-opera and pastoral roles. Except for a brief stint at Covent Garden in 1748, Beard acted exclusively at Drury Lane from 1743 until 1767. Despite his success, Beard and his family were often in financial difficulty. Finally, Beard began to go deaf in 1766 and retired from the stage until his death in

1791.

BENNETT, Elizabeth (1714-1791) – Gatty (*Bayes in Petticoats*)
Elizabeth Bennett was one of Garrick's workhorses. Her first
role was that of Mustacha in Fielding's *Opera of Operas* in 1733.
From 1735 to 1766 she had regular employment at Drury Lane
in hundreds of minor roles, inlcuding parts calling for singing
and dancing. Her specialties, according to Highfill, included
"gossips, flirts, pert maidservants, cast mistresses, and secondary
heroines in comedy." She managed to save her earnings, some
of which she donated to charitable causes throughout her life,
and lived comfortably after her retirement.

BRADSHAW, Mary (d. 1780) – First Lady ("Epilogue")
Mary Bradshaw made her professional debut at Lincoln's-Inn
Fields in January 1743 as Nell in Charles Coffey's *The Devil to
Pay*. She appeared again a few weeks later as Lucy in *The Beggar's Opera*. The same fall she made her first appearance at Drury
Lane as Kitty Pry in Garrick's *The Lying Valet*. Although she
played numerous roles at Drury Lane, her greatest successes
were in Garrick's own plays: the Farmer's Wife in *The Farmer's
Return from London* (1762), Mrs. Stockwell in *Neck or Nothing*
(1766), and Dorcas in *Cymon* (1767). By 1778 she had fallen into
minor specialty roles, and she was forced to apply for financial
aid from Garrick. Bradshaw was married to the boxkeeper at
Drury Lane, William Bradshaw.

CHAMPNESS, Samuel Thomas (d. 1803) – Cunning-Man (*Cunning-
Man*)
Like John Beard, Samuel Champness was a noted boy singer and
had oratorio parts written for him by Handel. Champness also
sang oratorios for much of his career. He was featured as a singer
at Drury Lane between 1748 and 1774, and he introduced Garrick's song "Hearts of Oak," set by William Boyce, in the afterpiece *Harlequin's Invasion* (1759). As an actor, Champness played
feature roles, such as Friar John in *Romeo and Juliet* and Hecate in
Macbeth. Although he retired from Drury Lane in 1774, he continued to sing oratorios until well into the 1780s.

CLIVE, Catherine (née Raftor) (1711-1785) – Mrs. Heidelberg

(*Clandestine Marriage*); Mrs. Hazard, Marcella (*Bayes in Petticoats*)
Known affectionately as "Kitty" for most of her career, Catherine Clive was the darling of Drury Lane theatre for over forty years. As a teenager, Catherine Raftor followed actors and was stage-struck; by 1728 she had been engaged as a singer at Drury Lane. Despite her singing talent, her debut role was as Bianca in *Othello*; later, she assumed the singing parts and primary comic roles that were to characterise her career. During the 1730s she was especially known for her interpretation of Polly in *The Beggar's Opera*. She married George Clive in 1733; they separated in 1735, and Clive remained married but single for the rest of her life. Clive accepted an engagement at Covent Garden in 1743, but returned to Drury Lane in 1746. She did not get along with the new manager, Garrick, the following season, but she continued to be the leading actress of the company, performing comedy, tragedy and opera with equal capability. Clive enjoyed moderate success as a playwright: aside from *Bayes in Petticoats*, she is known to have published two other afterpieces.

CROSS, Richard (d. 1760) – Prompter (*Bayes in Petticoats*)
An invaluable source of information about the London Stage from 1740 to 1760 comes from Richard Cross's diary. Cross was prompter during those years, first at Covent Garden, then at Drury Lane, and he kept meticulous records of performers, performances, and theatre accounts. Cross had begun his theatre career as an actor, playing hundreds of minor roles both at the Haymrket and Drury Lane between 1731 and 1738. Even during his tenure as prompter, Cross still appeared on stage in minor parts. In *Bayes in Petticoats*, Cross plays himself.

DODD, James William (1740?-1796) – Lord Minum ("Epilogue")
The son of a hairdresser, James William Dodd began his career as a country actor, playing roles such as Roderigo in *Othello*. He opened at Drury Lane in 1765 as Faddle in Edward Moore's *The Foundling*. Dodd played mostly comedies of manners and sentimental comedies, and specialised in fops and coxcombs. He was also celebrated for his portrayal of Cloten in *Cymbeline*.

DORMAN, Elizabeth (née Young) (d. 1773) – Third Lady ("Epilogue")

Elizabeth Dorman made her first appearance in 1758 as a replacement for Catherine Clive, playing Lucy in *The Beggar's Opera*. She joined Drury Lane permanently the following year, playing both her own roles and substitutes for first-line actors. Dorman was also known as a singer, and often sang at the Haymarket and King's Theatres.

HIPPISLEY, Elizabeth (fl. 1742-1769) – Miss Crotchet (*Bayes in Petticoats*)
Elizabeth Hippisley was the second daughter of John Hippisley, the actor who created the role of Macheath in *The Beggar's Opera*, and the younger sister of Jane Hippisley, also an actress. She made her stage debut at the outlawed Goodman's Fields Theatre in 1742, as Angelina in Colley Cibber's *Love Makes a Man*. From there, she moved to Covent Garden, where she played minor roles. In 1752 she moved to Drury Lane, where she premiered as Mrs. Trusty in Cibber's *The Provok'd Husband*. She retired from the stage in 1769, but the date of her death remains unknown.

HOLLAND, Charles (1732-1769) – Sir John Melvil (*Clandestine Marriage*)
Charles Holland made his debut at Drury Lane as Oroonoko in Thomas Southerne's adaptation of the Aphra Behn novel. He consciously modelled himself on Garrick's acting style; many regarded him as Garrick's protégé. He played dozens of leading roles at Drury Lane during his short career. After 1767, Holland managed the Theatre Royal in Bristol with William Powell; the two were celebrated there as an acting team. The success was short-lived, however: Holland contracted smallpox in 1769 and died, blind, in December of the same year. Garrick erected an elaborate monument to him.

KING, Thomas (1730-1805) – Lord Ogleby (*Clandestine Marriage*)
One of the leading actors at Drury Lane during Garrick's tenure, Thomas King had been tried out as the Herald in *King Lear*, and was the creator of Murza in Samuel Johnson's ill-fated *Mahomet and Irene* (1749). King left Drury Lane in 1750 to join Thomas Sheridan's Smock Alley Theatre in Dublin, where he became a specialist in prologue and epilogue delivery. King returned to Drury Lane in 1762 and, in addition to acting, wrote afterpieces

such as *Love at First Sight* (1763) and *Wit's Last Stake* (1769). King was initially reluctant to play Lord Ogleby, but the role brought him lasting fame. He was also celebrated as Garrick's foil in the *Shakespeare Jubilee* (1769) and as the creator of the role of Sir Peter Teazle in Sheridan's *School for Scandal* (1783). King bought shares in Sadler's Wells theatre, owning three-quarters of the patent until 1785.

LEE, Anna Sophia (d. 1770) – Mrs. Quaver ("Epilogue")
Anna Sophia Lee's career was often inextricably tied to the stormy career of her husband, John Lee. She began performing with him at Goodman's Fields in the late 1740s, but by 1750 she had begun her own appearances during the summer at Richmond. She played Juliet at Smock Alley in 1751, but followed her husband to Canongate Concert Hall, Edinburgh and later Bath. She joined Drury Lane in 1762 on a contract for six seasons, and supplemented this activity with summer seasons at James Love's theatre in Richmond beginning in 1765. Lee died at Bath in 1770.

LEE, John (1725-1781) – Traverse (*Clandestine Marriage*)
John Lee specialised in Shakespearian roles, making his Drury Lane debut as Hotspur in *Henry IV, part One* in 1746. During the 1746-47 season he played Shakespearian parts both at Drury Lane and at Goodman's Fields. Lee was known to be irascible, and had rocky relationships with most of his fellow actors. He deserted Drury Lane for Covent Garden in 1749, but Garrick threatened legal action and had him return to finish his contract, which expired in 1752. He served one season at Smock Alley Theatre, but at the end of 1752 he had taken over management of Canongate Concert Hall in Edinburgh. He entered into legal wranglings over the ownership of the property, and was jailed for two months in 1756. Between 1757 and 1762 he played at Smock Alley, Bath, Winchester, Edinburgh, and, finally, Drury Lane. His last engagement was at the Theatre Royal, Bath, in 1768.

LOVE, James (née Dance) (1721-1774) – Serjeant Flower (*Clandestine Marriage*)
Poet, playwright, actor, and theatre manager, James Dance was

born to an accomplished artistic family. His brother Nathaniel Dance, also known as Nathaniel Holland, was a portrait painter; his brother George was an architect and is famous for his monochrome portraits of figures such as James Boswell and Joseph Haydn. As a playwright, Dance is best remembered for his adaptation of Samuel Richardson's *Pamela* (1741); he also wrote the afterpieces *The Witches* (1762) and *The Hermit* (1766). He began his acting career in 1746 at Covent Garden, playing Bayes in *The Rehearsal*. He was hired at Drury Lane in 1762, but his relations with Garrick became strained after he refused to promote one of Garrick's protoges at the New Theatre on the Green in Richmond, which Dance had managed since 1765. Dance adopted the surname "Love" in 1751, after the name of his mistress, Catherine L'Amour.

MILLS, Theodosia (fl. 1748-1794) – Trusty (*Clandestine Marriage*); Second Lady ("Epilogue")
One of Drury Lane's many supporting players, Theodosia Mills began her Drury Lane career in 1752 in Buckingham's *The Rehearsal*. She appeared in hundreds of minor parts, many not even mentioned on the playbills. She remained at the bottom of the actor's pay scale (2s. 6d. *per diem*) during most of her tenure at Drury Lane. She followed George Colman to Covent Garden in 1767, at an increased salary of 3s. 4d. She left Covent Garden for the Haymarket in 1770. Sometime after 1771, she is known to have been Colman's mistress.

MINORS (or MYNERS), Sybilla (later Mrs. John Walker) (1723-1802) – Miss Giggle (*Bayes in Petticoats*)
Nothing is known of Sybilla Minors' early life or her parentage. She premiered at Drury Lane in 1741 as one of the Gypsy Women in *The Fortune Tellers*. According to Highfill, her specialties included "hoydenish country girls, frisky ingenues, pert servants, occasional singing parts, and minor tragic roles." After her marriage to John Walker, the couple left for Dublin, and eventually settled at Covent Garden.

MOODY, John (née Cochrane) (1727-1812) – Sir Patrick Mahony ("Epilogue")
Born in Cork, John Cochrane changed his name to Moody on

his arrival in England to disguise his Irish roots. He left for Jamaica in 1745 and there joined an acting company, where he specialised in Shakesperian roles. By 1759 he had returned to England, and was playing in Portsmouth when Garrick discovered him. He specialised in comic characters, and was particularly noted for playing Irish. He remained faithful to Garrick until the end of Garrick's career, and remained at Drury Lane until 1796. In later years he was accused of sloppy acting, and appeared less frequently; his last roles were at Covent Garden early in the 19th century.

MOZEEN, Thomas (1720?-1768) – Tom (*Bayes in Petticoats*)
Thomas Mozeen was of French parentage, although he was born in England. He had initially studied law, but he was attracted to the stage, and first appeared in 1743 as Stanley in *Richard III* under Theophilus Cibber at Lincoln's-Inn Fields. In 1745 he made his debut at Drury Lane as Pembroke in *King John*. Mozeen played Smock Alley with his wife Mary in 1748-49, returning to Drury Lane in 1750. He left Drury Lane again in 1764. His final engagement was at Covent Garden in 1767-68, though he did not live to the end of the season. Mozeen wrote several afterpieces, many of them unperformed and all unpublished.

PALMER, John (1728-1768) – Brush (*Clandestine Marriage*)
John Palmer was known as "Gentleman John," partly because of his stiff, formal demeanour, and partly to distinguish him from his more raucous contemporary, "Plausible Jack" Palmer (1744-1798). Palmer played a number of leading roles, but was criticised for his lack of variety in his acting. He married the more accomplished Hannah Mary Pritchard in 1761, and the couple often acted together, as they did in *The Clandestine Marriage*. Palmer died accidentally in 1768 from a mistaken overdose of a sleeping-draught.

PALMER, Hannah Mary Pritchard (later Mrs. Lloyd) (1739-1781) – Fanny Sterling (*Clandestine Marriage*)
Hannah Mary Pritchard was the youngest daughter of celebrated tragedian Hannah Pritchard and the actor William Pritchard. At the age of 16 she was put under the tutelage of Garrick in acting and of Georges St-Jean Noverre in dancing. She made her Lon-

don debut as Juliet in 1756, opposite her mother as Lady Capulet. She remained a first- and second-line actress throughout her career, although she always laboured under the shadow of her more famous mother. She retired from the stage after her second marriage to importer and stock-jobber Maurice Lloyd.

PLYM, Miss (fl. 1753-1773) – Chambermaid (*Clandestine Marriage*)
A "Miss Plym" is first noted in 1753 at Bath, mentioned in a piece of doggerel by John Lee. She made her Drury Lane debut as Viola in *Twelfth Night*. Although she played mainly minor and supporting roles, she did appear as Hero in *Much Ado About Nothing* and as Margery Pinchwife in Wycherly's *The Country Wife*. She seems to have retired after the 1766-67 season. She became the mistress of the Marquis of Clanricarde, but is not mentioned in his will.

POPE, Jane (1744?-1818) – Miss Betsey Sterling (*Clandestine Marriage*)
Jane Pope began her 52-year stage career at the age of 12 in Garrick's farce, *Lilliput*. Her first adult role was Corinna in Sir John Vanbrugh's *The Confederacy* in 1759. She created the role of Polly Honeycombe in Colman's afterpiece, and had leading parts throughout the century. In later years, she was known for playing Mrs. Heidelberg, a part that George III called for in 1801. She also created the title role in R.B. Sheridan's *The Duenna*. Pope retired in 1808 because of failing memory.

POWELL, William (c. 1735-1769) – Lovewell (*Clandestine Marriage*)
William Powell's background was originally in business, but he was introduced to Garrick by Charles Holland and made his stage debut as Philaster in George Colman's adaptation of the Beaumont and Fletcher comedy. Powell became part manager, with Holland, of the Theatre Royal in Bristol, but was frequently ill after 1768. He died of pneumonia in 1769, apparently as a result of throwing himself on damp grass after a cricket match.

SHUTER, Edward (1728-1776) – Witling (*Bayes in Petticoats*)
Edward "Ned" Shuter's comic talents were first noticed by provincial theatre manager Thomas Chapman, who cast him as the

cook in a performance of Henry Carey's burlesque *Chrononho-tonthologos* in 1744. Shuter played at Goodman's Fields from 1746-47, and joined Foote's Haymarket company when Goodman's Fields was closed by the Licencing Act. Garrick hired Shuter during his first season as Drury Lane manager, and his career lasted until Garrick's retirement. He was especially known for his low comic roles, particularly Falstaff. In later years he suffered from excessive drinking, often becoming disorderly and unable to act.

SIMPSON, Elizabeth (fl. 1744-1774) – Miss Sidle (*Bayes in Petticoats*)
A number of actresses known as Miss/Mrs. Simpson (or Simson) appeared at Drury Lane during Garrick's tenure, and Elizabeth Simpson cannot now be identified with any great certainty. The "Miss Simpson" who played Miss Sidle in *Bayes in Petticoats* was known for playing maids and eccentrics, and also specialised in pantomime roles.

THOMAS, Miss (fl. 1752-1776) – Miranda (*Bayes in Petticoats*)
The "Miss Thomas" who sang Miranda in *Bayes in Petticoats* was possibly a pupil of Christopher Pepusch, composer and arranger. She was known mainly as a singer, appearing at the Haymarket, Maylebone Gardens and Ranelagh Gardens, as well as at Drury Lane. After 1762 she appeared exclusively at Covent Garden.

TOOGOOD, Sarah (d. 1755) – Miss Dawdle (*Bayes in Petticoats*)
Nothing is known of Sarah Toogood's early career, but she had been performing minor roles at Drury Lane throughout the 1740s as both an actor and a dancer. In 1750 she appeared as Colombine in the Burney/Woodward pantomime *Queen Mab*; later she appeared in roles such as Gipsey in *The Beaux' Stratagem* and Dainty Fidget in *The Country Wife*. Cross's diary records her death date as 1755. Sarah Toogood left a ten-year-old daughter who performed with Lalauze's dance troupe, but who disappears from the stage records after 1759.

VERNON, Joseph (1738?-1782) – Colin (*Cunning-Man*)
Joseph Vernon began his career as a singer, first appearing at Drury Lane in 1751 in Thomas Arne's masque *Alfred*. He sang tenor parts at Drury Lane and also acted in comedy. Vernon's

clandestine marriage was one of the first to be prosecuted under the Marriage Act, and this action forced him from Drury Lane for a number of years. He played in Dublin and occasionally sang at Vauxhall. He returned to Drury Lane in 1762, and played there until his retirement in 1781. Before his death the following year, he compiled the *New London and Country Songster, or, a Bouquet of Vocal Music.*

WOODWARD, Henry (1714-1777) – Witling (*Bayes in Petticoats*)
Apprenticed as a tallow chandler, Henry Woodward abandoned his trade in 1729 to join John Rich's child company, the Lilliputian Troupe of Lun. His first appearance was as Robin of Bagshot in an all-child production of *The Beggar's Opera.* Woodward appeared regularly at Goodman's-Fields from 1730-1736, and then afterwards at Lincoln's-Inn Fields until its closure in 1737. His Drury Lane debut was as Feeble in *Henry IV, part Two,* and he quickly established himself as the leading comedian of his time. Except for a season at Smock Alley in 1747-48, he remained at Drury Lane until 1758. During that time he not only created numerous comic roles, he also wrote successful pantomimes, such as *Harelquin Ranger* (1751), *The Genii* and *Queen Mab* (1752), and *Fortunatus* (1753). Although Garrick regarded him as indispensable, Woodward was persuaded by Spranger Barry to open a new theatre in Dublin. Initially a success, the Crow St. Theatre soon ran into financial trouble, and closed in 1762. Woodward returned to London, but played at Covent Garden until 1777; his last role was Stephano in *The Tempest.*

YATES, Richard (1706?-1796) – Sterling (*Clandestine Marriage*)
Richard Yates's first recorded stage appearance was as Lord Place in Fielding's *Pasquin* at the Haymarket in 1735. He joined Drury Lane in 1739 and created the roles of Mrs. Jewkes in Dance's *Pamela* and Dick in Garrick's *The Lying Valet.* He married fellow comedian Mary Ann Graham in 1756, and she later superseded her husband in popularity. However, Yates continued to create leading comic roles, and was one of Drury Lane's leading actors. He was especially noted for playing Shakespearian clowns. He followed Colman to Covent Garden in 1767, but returned to Drury Lane in 1775.